The Beatles Movies

The Beatles Movies

Bob Neaverson

CASSELL

London and Washington

Rethinking British Cinema
Series Editor: Pam Cook

This series is dedicated to innovative approaches to British cinema. It expands the parameters of debate, shedding new light on areas such as gender and sexuality, audiences, ethnicity, stars, visual style, genre, music and sound. Moving beyond narrow definitions of national cinema, the series celebrates the richness and diversity of British film culture.

Pam Cook lectures in film at the University of East Anglia and is editor of *The Cinema Book*.

Cassell
Wellington House
125 Strand
London WC2R 0BB

PO Box 605
Herndon, VA 20172

First published 1997

British Library Cataloguing-in-Publication Data
A catalogue record for this book is available from the British Library.

ISBN 0 304 33796 X (hardback)
    0 304 33797 8 (paperback)

Typeset by Ben Cracknell Studios
Printed and bound in Great Britain by Biddles Ltd,
Guildford and King's Lynn

Contents

Preface

I was born in August 1967, far too late to hear the Beatles' music the first time around. The first conscious memory I have of hearing their music was when I was around four years old, when my aunty played *The Beatles' Hits* EP (by then almost a decade old) at my grandparents' house. Between 1978 and 1983 I was away at boarding school in Cambridgeshire. During those years pop music became, for many of us, infinitely more important than it probably should have been, serving somehow as a source of comfort, rebellion, catharsis and escapism which, to this day, I'm still unable to explain fully or articulately. Although they had been finished for some eight years by that time, the most endearing records I heard were by the Beatles and, from the age of eleven onwards I was hooked. In 1979 the BBC screened a series of Beatles movies, the first of which, if my memory serves, was *A Hard Day's Night*.

When you're eleven you don't sit down and analyse why something fascinates you: things either capture your imagination or they don't. Retrospectively, I suppose it was because the Beatles did everything that we couldn't do, said everything we couldn't say and were everything that we couldn't be. They answered back to the forces of authority, they dressed differently, had their own code of idiolect, were by turns amusing, witty, sarcastic, profound and compassionate. Then there were the songs. Seventeen years later, I still think that *A Hard Day's Night* is the most exciting piece of pop committed to disc. What's more, although at that age it was impossible to see through the illusionism of it all, the Beatles' onscreen personas were charged with such authenticity that it was impossible to believe that they weren't like this 'in real life'. It was, of course, one of the most intricately and self-consciously 'crafted' films of its time, but two film degrees, around fifty viewings, years of reading and studying and listening later, and its fiction still exudes a remarkable sense of realism.

My first research for this book was undertaken when writing a thesis on *Magical Mystery Tour*, carried out at the University of East Anglia towards an MA in Film Studies. The original idea for the thesis was that it would cover the entire spectrum of the Beatles' film work. On the sound advice of my supervisors, this idea was rejected as over-ambitious, and I decided to stick to a single movie. This was no great sacrifice, however, not least because it allowed me greater scope to analyse what I consider to be the most overlooked work in the Beatles' canon. That said, this book has enabled me to fulfil that original ambition, and to examine both critically and historically an area of film history which, in my opinion, has been ignored for far too long. Writing this book has been an enormously enjoyable and enlightening experience, not least because of the interest, support and advice which I have received from a vast number of people, all of whom, in one way or another, have given freely of their time and experience to help.

For being such a patient and helpful series editor I am indebted to Pam Cook, who was also instrumental in getting this book off the ground. My thanks also to Jane Greenwood and Alan Worth at Cassell for their faith and assistance with this project. Along with Pam, Kevin Donnelly read through the drafts and provided excellent and intelligent comments on work in progress, and I am most grateful for his expert advice on the relationship between music and film. Thanks too to John Street who, besides Pam and Kevin, acted as an advisor on my original thesis, some of which has been adapted for this publication.

When I embarked upon this book, I was determined that it should contain as much original material as possible, and that it should include comments culled from new interviews conducted with as many reliable and informed sources as I could find. There are, after all, too many 'scissors and paste' Beatles books on the market already. I am therefore extremely grateful to all the people who agreed to be interviewed for this work, including Dick Lester, Joe McGrath, Gavrik Losey, Victor Spinetti and Denis O'Dell. A special word of thanks to Denis, who was kind enough to discuss his experiences of the Beatles' films for the first time. I hope I have done your inspired answers and insights the justice they deserve. I would also like to thank my friend and ex-boss Peta Button for helping me to track down potential interviewees, and for showing such supportive interest in my work.

Putting together a book of this nature inevitably means researching a variety of resource materials. As well as original interviews, much of the information used for this work has been culled from films, television documentaries, archive footage, books, magazines, periodicals, sound-tracks, programmes, fanzines and other items of Beatles memorabilia.

I am very grateful to the BFI and the National Newspaper Library at Colindale for their help with this project, as well as to my friends Trevor Howsam and Robin Hammerton, who were good enough to entrust to me valuable items of memorabilia. Thanks also to the Beatles discographer, Neville Stannard (author of the excellent *Long and Winding Road* and *Working Class Heroes*), who was extremely helpful in supplying me with both materials and advice on the Beatles' recorded output. I am also most grateful to Jeremy Neech at Apple for his help with the illustrations.

When you are stuck in the darkest corners of Norwich, you have to find somewhere to stay when you spend time researching in London. Thanks to all the people (too numerous to mention) who have helped me out, especially one of my oldest friends, Mat Daniels, who was also a constant source of encouragement in the writing of this book. Finally, I would like to thank my family for being so supportive of this endeavour, and especially my wife, Bodil, who provided constant encouragement beyond the call of duty. I dedicate this book to her.

Bob Neaverson
1996

Introduction
The Long and Winding Road:
Towards a Beatles Film History

The popular version of the Beatles' history has been recycled so often by the British media that it has become part of our national folklore. It has become a well-loved fairytale, an ultimate 'rags to riches' morality story in which four working-class boys overcome poverty, personal tragedy, and indifference to become the world's most important and well loved pop group. Into the bargain, they give the Yanks a good hiding and prove beyond all reasonable doubt that Britain is culturally superior in the world of popular music.

There are of course other, more searching and critical histories of the group and their artistic output, but more often than not the development of their career is reduced to a series of events, charted (rather than assessed) as a highly selective sequence of hiatuses and watersheds, documented as if somehow divorced from their original social, political and artistic contexts. The Beatles appear on *The Ed Sullivan Show*, the Beatles play Shea Stadium, the Beatles get the MBE, the Beatles go to India to meditate, and so forth. Serious studies have been almost exclusively concerned with the Beatles' songwriting and recording career. While this is understandable (the Beatles *were*, after all, primarily a groundbreaking songwriting and recording unit), there are facets of the group's career which have been overlooked for too long.

This book hopes to go some way towards redressing the balance by historically and critically reassessing what must surely be the most neglected aspect of the Beatles' output, the group's films. To the best of my knowledge, no single work has dealt exclusively and/or seriously with their films, which have largely been treated as little more than a historical footnote by writers, critics and film historians alike. Yet throughout the sixties, film was central to the Beatles' career and, although that career was relatively short lived (their main body of recorded work spanned a mere eight years), no less than five of their major record releases were augmented by films: *A Hard Day's Night* (1964), *Help!* (1965), *Magical Mystery Tour* (TVM, 1967), *Yellow Submarine* (1968) and *Let It Be* (1970).

That the films should, with a few notable exceptions, have been so neglected within film studies is possibly the result of a number of critical biases prevalent within much of the discipline's methodological schemata. In particular, the generic status of the pop musical, to which the films for the most part belong, has, for reasons largely unknown to me, never garnered much interest within British film history and theory. In addition, much film history still favours an exclusively auteurist approach, and, since the five Beatles movies were made by four different directors (or sets of directors), they do not form part of an auteurist canon. It is perhaps unsurprising, then, that Dick Lester's films, *A Hard Day's Night* (1964) and *Help!* (1965), have received more critical attention than the other three movies and, while this is not to denigrate the importance of these works, the bias of approach inherent in much film history has, I am certain, been at least partly instrumental in their critical and historical prioritization. Indeed, it is interesting to speculate upon the current critical position of the films had they all been directed by a single 'auteur'. They may not have become the most talked about films of their period, but my suspicion is that they would have received much more attention than they have done.

These problems of theoretical discipline have been compounded by practical external factors concerning the availability and dissemination of the films, and despite the recent upsurge in the group's popularity (as I write this, in early 1996, the Beatles' public profile has been immeasurably raised by the television release of their *Anthology* documentary series and two of three double CD packages), the movies have, for the most part, received scant exhibition of late. Although the Lester films have had frequent television screenings and video releases, the other movies have been less fortunate. *Let It Be*, for example, has not been seen on terrestrial British television for over a decade and has yet to receive a British sell-through video release. The other two films have fared little better, and although *Magical Mystery Tour* was issued on home video in the late eighties (complete with a remastered soundtrack), it was soon deleted and remains unavailable.

Moreover, it must be said that the position of the Beatles' movies in film history has not been aided by the poor commercial and critical reception of the group's subsequent 'solo' forays into film acting, production and direction. Although in the early eighties George Harrison's Handmade production outfit was regarded as a potential saviour of the British film industry, his interests in the company have since been terminated in an explosion of legal battles. McCartney's solo attempt to script and star in a feature film, *Give My Regards to Broad Street* (1984), was also a resounding commercial and critical flop. Moreover, Starr's attempts to involve himself in film-making have brought little acclaim, and despite a crowning performance in *That'll Be the Day* (1973) his forays into film acting have rarely matched his indisputable potential, and his singular attempt at direction, *Born to Boogie* (1972), went largely unnoticed. His venture into film production, *Son of Dracula* (1972), fared little better. Add to these factors the Beatles' own lack of interest in discussing the movies and/or their out-of-hand dismissal of them (particularly by the ever acerbic Lennon), and the recipe for their relative obscurity in film history is complete.

Although the group had varying levels of financial and creative involvement in the making of their films (their input ranging from detached indifference to total immersion), the Beatles movies occupy an important position, not only within the context of their own artistic and financial development, but, from a broader perspective, within the development of British and American film and television culture as a whole.

For example, the Beatles' films were (along with their recordings and live appearances) central to the creation and maintenance of the social phenomenon of 'Beatlemania'. After all, cinema was the only medium through which the group's ever-changing music and meticulously crafted array of 'images' could be fully articulated on a global scale. Without film, the Beatles' global popularity would not and could not have existed to anything like the same degree.

Moreover, in economic terms the movies were influential in the development of cinema's multimedia marketing campaigns. Although primitive by today's standards, the Beatles pop musicals, along with the

James Bond cycle, were amongst the most successful series of pre-seventies films to act as large-scale advertisements for 'tie-in' products external to the film-going experience.

Finally, from formal and ideological perspectives, the movies are of considerable film historical significance. Dick Lester's *A Hard Day's Night* was one of the first pop musicals to represent pop stars in anything other than a clean-cut, conformist, one-dimensional manner. On a purely formal level, it was the first film of its kind to fully realize and systematically deploy the illustrative potential of pop music, frequently rejecting the established precedent of performance-based musical sequences in favour of those which married entire songs with non-performance-based conceptual action. This radical break with previous generic conventions formed an aesthetic precedent which encompassed both the group's subsequent films (*Help!*, *Magical Mystery Tour* and *Yellow Submarine*) and promos (such as *Strawberry Fields Forever*), non-Beatles-related pop films and, perhaps most profoundly, the medium of contemporary pop video. Moreover, the Beatles were also the first pop group to become personally involved in the mechanical process of film-making and, despite its huge critical failure, *Magical Mystery Tour* remains the only film to have been written, financed, produced and directed by a pop group. More importantly, it was the first pop musical to break so wholeheartedly with the constraints of narrative logic, again setting an aesthetic precedent for a number of subsequent pop movies.

The intentions of this book are essentially twofold. It will provide the reader with a historical insight into the production, marketing and reception of the Beatles films, whilst also facilitating a critical evaluation of the texts themselves. In so doing, I want to evaluate and reinstate the films' significance, both within the group's own career/canon and within film history generally. My approach, which is largely chronological, is to assess the movies from a number of different perspectives, considering their formal and ideological properties, marketing and reception within the context of sixties pop musicals, non-pop-oriented films, and British television. I will examine the social, artistic and ideological influences of the films and, in the final chapter, the influence of the Beatles movies on subsequent productions. A chapter is devoted to each film, with slightly more emphasis placed upon *Magical Mystery Tour*, perhaps the most formally interesting of the films. It is also the film in which the group had the greatest personal involvement, and it is far and away the most historically neglected artefact in the group's canon, its resounding critical failure making it a fascinating anomaly in the Beatles' history and opening a plethora of debates surrounding its reception. However, before we survey the films, an important question must first be considered. Why did the Beatles make films and what was the underlying economic rationale behind them?

I believe the answer to be twofold. First, and most obviously, making films for international distribution was the easiest and most practical way to ensure consistent global exposure, and thus to generate maximum box-office and/or television exhibition revenue. Film production provided a more efficient means of public exposure than touring or making exclusive television appearances throughout the world, and was ultimately less time-consuming for a group of international stature. Moreover, the commercial and ideological importance of making films became even more pronounced in the wake of their unwillingness to continue their previously gruelling schedule of such performances. After their 1966 appearance in Candlestick Park, they declined to tour and, as Mark Lewisohn's *Complete Beatles Chronicle* testifies, they subsequently made only a limited number of exclusive television appearances. Indeed, according to Lewisohn, the group made only four exclusive British television appearances in 1966. In 1963, they had made a staggering thirty-seven.[1]

Making films and internationally exhibited television appearances therefore became of paramount importance and when, in 1967, the BBC invited the group to perform as British representatives for the world's first global satellite link-up, *Our World*, they were keen to oblige, even composing an exclusive song ('All You Need is Love') for the event, which was seen by an international audience of over 200 million. As Beatles road managers/assistants Mal Evans and Neil Aspinall maintained in 1967, just before the release of *Magical Mystery Tour*: 'The obvious alternative to touring was to produce their own occasional television shows which could be seen all over the world, in countries they had visited for concert tours as well as new countries they'd never got around to.'[2] Indeed, it is tempting to make a comparison with the group's most serious transatlantic competitor, Elvis Presley, who, by the early sixties, had also [albeit temporarily] forsaken live concert tours for a career in globally exhibited pop musicals such as *G.I. Blues* (1960), *Girls! Girls! Girls!* (1962) and *Fun in Acapulco* (1963). Whether the Beatles, or their advisers, based their career moves on those of Presley is a question that will perhaps remain unanswered. Nevertheless, despite the formal and ideological differences between the Beatles and the Presley films, it is important to acknowledge that their underlying economic rationale was ultimately identical.

Second, whilst the films clearly had the potential to generate 'direct' revenue from box office receipts and television exhibition rights, they also facilitated, to varying degrees, the sales of a range of tie-in products, encompassing such items as soundtrack records, sheet music, novelizations, gift books and any number of other novelty accessories. In order to understand the underlying economic rationale and generic mechanisms of the Beatles' four pop musicals (and indeed their one generic anomaly, the *Let It Be* documentary), we must first consider them in relation to other, extra-textual elements.

Thomas Schatz, in his fascinating article *The New Hollywood*, discusses the manner by which commercial American cinema has become increasingly dominated by tie-in merchandising, endorsing the idea that a contemporary production such as *Batman* (1989) is 'best understood as a multi-media, multi-market sales campaign.'[3] Although Schatz sees this trend as having evolved largely from the multi-media success of such seventies Hollywood productions as *Jaws* (1975) and *Star Wars* (1977), the exploitation of tie-in merchandising is neither a new nor exclusively American phenomenon, and I would maintain that it is also possible to view the Beatles films as influential, if primitive, multi-media production concepts designed to facilitate the merchandising of products external to, and beyond, box office revenue generated by the film-going experience. This practice had, however, been implemented (albeit in a more modest manner) long before the release of any of the Beatles films, and indeed before the rise of the pop musicals of the late fifties, through sales of soundtrack records and sheet music. However, with the appearance of the first British and American pop musicals in the mid to late fifties, the practice of concurrently marketing a range of related goods became standard within the genre. For example, Tommy Steele's 1960 vehicle, *Tommy the Toreador*, was designed as a commercial package which included, as well as the obligatory soundtrack record and sheet music, such diverse items as toreador outfits, puppets, bath mats and knitting patterns.[4]

However, although the Beatles certainly didn't invent this exploitative concept, their film productions followed a similar economic strategy, with the sale of soundtrack material obviously highest on the agenda. Indeed, all their films (produced and/or distributed through either Apple or United Artists) were released in tandem with soundtrack albums, EPs or singles which included for the most part music taken from, and frequently written specifically for, their contemporary film releases. Of these, *A Hard Day's Night* provided the richest source of soundtrack spin-offs and, while the British release of the film (premiered on 6 July 1964) was accompanied by the concurrent release of the soundtrack and single of the same name, there were also a number of other related record releases. The single 'Can't Buy Me Love' was released shortly before the film in March 1964, and there were two EP releases, although only one, 'Extracts from the Film "A Hard Day's Night"', contained music taken from the film. The other, which was not released into the American market, consisted of songs from the soundtrack album which were not featured in the movie.

Such an approach usually fulfilled a mutually beneficial role for ever changing film and record production companies (in the Beatles' case, often different divisions of the same company) since one medium helped to generate profits for the other. Moreover, despite the fact that all five Beatles films are vastly different in form (compare, for example, the cinema direct of *Let It Be* with the fantasy animation of *Yellow Submarine*), the common thread of all the films' narratives (indeed of all pop films of the fifties and sixties) is the insertion of contemporary recordings into their discourse.

While selling specific records (and their sheet music) was obviously an important consideration for potential product sales, the films, like the vehicles of other contemporary pop stars, also generated the extensive sale of other tie-in products, such as Dell's glossy film books, Sheffield's *Yellow Submarine* clocks, or Jaymar's *Yellow Submarine* jigsaw puzzles. Such artefacts were manufactured by agreement with the distributors and/or the Beatles' own film rights/royalties outlet, Subafilms, an offshoot of the Beatles' management company, Northern End Music Stores Enterprises (NEMS), set up by manager Brian Epstein in 1964 to deal with the group's film projects.[5] And, although unquantifiable in sales terms, the films also helped to sell other non-film-related Beatles products, such as jackets, Cuban heeled boots, board games and wigs. Again, such products were manufactured by agreement with two merchandising copyright outlets, Stramsact and Seltaeb, companies initially set up by agreement with Epstein in 1963 and 1964 respectively.[6]

However, these two companies did not, at least for the Beatles and Epstein, secure the huge profits which they promised, and millions of pounds of potential earnings were lost as a result of two central factors. First, the deals which Epstein set up with the two companies were unfavourable, with NEMS initially receiving only 10 per cent of the licence fees paid to the companies for the use of the Beatles' name and likeness. Epstein has often been criticized for failing to establish a more favourable deal with the licensing outlets, but such criticism seems unfair when one considers that the economic potential of pop-related merchandise was a largely unknown quantity in the early sixties. Beatlemania had produced a hysteria which transcended ordinary admiration and excitement, triggering a vast market for virtually any product which sported the group's name or likeness. Although one could argue that Epstein committed the cardinal managerial sin of failing to predict future pop trends, the speed with which Beatlemania gripped the global marketplace was completely unprecedented. As former Apple film chief Denis O'Dell rightly maintains, 'Nobody knew the strength of it.'[7] Secondly, earnings were further diminished by the availability of totally unlicensed Beatles-based products (which reached unprecedented heights during the first wave of Beatlemania), because unscrupulous manufacturers and dealers could easily avoid prosecutions over copyright infringements by simply spelling the group's name as 'Beetles'. Indeed, as Philip Norman maintains, by 1964 the hunger for Beatles-related ephemera was such that 'the vaguest representation of insects, of guitars or little mop-headed men, had the power to sell anything'.[8] While it is impossible to quantify the degree to which these products affected the sale of 'official' goods, one thing is certain: just as Schatz rightly sees today's youthful audiences as multimarket, multimedia consumers, so too were those who went to see the Beatles' films.

Following Epstein's death in August 1967, the Beatles did everything in their power to control their own means of production. Although the group's first two films were funded and released through the American giant, United Artists, they were quick to realize the potential economic and artistic benefits of self-ownership and, from summer 1967, they began to set up a group of companies which would eventually comprise the divisions of Apple Corps, their own self-financed production and management company.

As well as serving as a means of avoiding the then exorbitant rates of capital gains tax, the formation of Apple theoretically allowed the Beatles the freedom to invest in a vast range of different divisions: a record label, a tailoring and clothing retail division, a publishing outlet, an electronics division and a film division. The films division, Apple Films, was headed by producer Denis O'Dell and was specifically designed to finance and produce their increasingly important film and television ventures. The formation of their own film production company had a dual role. First, and most obviously, it meant potentially higher returns; second, it meant that the Beatles retained a greater degree of economic and artistic control over their product output. *Magical Mystery Tour* was the first Beatles production to be credited to Apple Films. Because of contractual and professional complications, their later productions, *Let It Be* and *Yellow Submarine*, were not totally financed, distributed and/or produced by their film division. Thus *Magical Mystery Tour* can be viewed as the single most 'unadulterated' production in the Beatles canon, a film which they personally controlled at almost every level of its evolution. However, the long and winding road to *Magical Mystery Tour* began three years earlier, with *A Hard Day's Night*.

Notes

1. Lewisohn, 1992, p. 355. However, it should be noted that British audiences were also treated to a screening of the non-exclusive Anglo-American co-production, *The Beatles at Shea Stadium*, a forty-minute concert documentary made predominantly for American audiences but premiered in Britain in March 1966.
2. Evans and Aspinall, 1967, p. 6.
3. Schatz, in Collins, Radner and Collins, 1993, p. 32.
4. 'Renter's News' in *Kine Weekly*, no. 2731, 28 January 1960, p. 17.
5. Friede, Titone and Weiner, 1981, p. 206.
6. For more information on the formation of these companies, see Norman, 1981, pp. 202–3.
7. Denis O'Dell, interviewed by the author, 30 April 1996.
8. Norman, 1981, p. 201.

I

You Can Do That!
A Hard Day's Night

In 1962, the Beatles released their first single in Britain. It was called 'Love Me Do' and, although it only reached number 17 in the '*Record Retailer*' charts, its modest success heralded a major break in a pop tradition that had previously been almost exclusively dominated by American and British balladeers and London-based groups. By 1963 teenage 'Beatlemania' (a phrase originally coined by the *Daily Mirror*[1]) had become widespread in Britain, and by the end of the year the Beatles had produced Britain's first million-selling album ('With the Beatles') and three enormously successful number one singles. Although British artistes had not previously achieved any significant success in the US, by 2 March 1964 – the first day of shooting for *A Hard Day's Night* – the group had also 'conquered' America, within a month occupying all top five positions in the *Billboard* charts.

The appearance of the first Beatles film came, in retrospect, as little surprise. Since the arrival of such British pop stars as Tommy Steele and Cliff Richard in the late fifties, the pop musical had become commonplace in British cinema. After the success of the American-made Bill Haley vehicle, *Rock Around the Clock*, in 1956, British producers had been keen to capitalize on the increasingly 'disposable' income of the emerging teenage market, creating a spate of pop star vehicles such as *The Tommy Steele Story* (1957), *The Duke Wore Jeans* (1958) and *Expresso Bongo* (1959). However, despite a minority of more generously budgeted and professionally produced Cliff Richard films in the early sixties, most pop musicals were made as low budget, exploitative 'quickies' intended to capitalize on the rock and roll 'craze' by generating maximum profits for the lowest possible investment.[2] Although by 1964 it was becoming clear that rock and roll was an increasingly bankable phenomenon, the production history of *A Hard Day's Night* reeks of the same exploitative approach.

Although shooting for the film began in March 1964, its preparation commenced some six months earlier, in October 1963, when Beatles manager Brian Epstein met with the independent American producer, Walter Shenson, who had been appointed by United Artists' European production head, George H. Ornstein. At this point in their career, the Beatles, although an enormous phenomenon in Britain, had yet fully to establish themselves within the American market. The group had not yet attained the superstar status which followed their groundbreaking television appearance on *The Ed Sullivan Show* in February 1964.[3] So the project was initially envisaged by the American-owned company as little more than another low-budget exploitation picture which would capitalize on the group's fleeting success with the teenage market and, most importantly, provide its record label with a lucrative tie-in soundtrack album.[4] Indeed, as Shenson later revealed, the company was only interested in making a Beatles film 'for the express purpose of having a soundtrack album', and he was given no other guidelines apart from an instruction to make a film with 'enough new songs by the Beatles for a new album'.[5]

For their part, the Beatles were initially sceptical about appearing in pop musicals, and not without reason. After all, not only did they lack any formal acting experience, they had also seen their former hero, Elvis Presley, throw his 'beautiful image as a pop superman clean out of the window'[6] by forsaking his more obvious talents to undertake a career in movies. Worse, they were unimpressed by the flimsy, contrived B-movie quality of British pop films, and felt that theirs would be no different. As Lennon said to Epstein prior to shooting, 'We don't fancy being Bill Haley and the Bellhops, Brian. We're not going to walk in and out of endless studios bumping into Helen Shapiro and Mark Wynter and saying "Hi there" to Alan Freeman.'[7] More importantly, things were going extraordinarily well as they were, so why put their heads on the chopping block by interacting with a world of which they knew nothing? Did they really need to risk making fools of themselves and destroying their hitherto impeccable track record?

Because of their initial lack of confidence in the film's profitability, United Artists' budget for *A Hard Day's Night* was set at a modest £200,000, with the Beatles receiving £20,000, plus 7½ per cent of the profits.[8] According to former press officer Tony Barrow, United Artists had expected to pay up to three times this percentage, but because of their initial scepticism over the film's success, they 'weren't particularly overjoyed at their good fortune'.[9] Having drawn up the agreement, and arranged for the group to write and record six new songs for the soundtrack, Shenson had to decide what kind of film to make. On meeting the Beatles, he had tentatively decided that the film should be a musical comedy and, with their agreement, hired American ex-patriate Richard Lester as director.

In many ways, Lester was an obvious choice both for the Beatles and for Shenson. He had already worked with Shenson on the comedy *The Mouse on the Moon* (1963), and as a former musician and director of the trad boom musical, *It's Trad Dad* (1962), was well attuned to contemporary pop sensibilities. Indeed, Lester had heard the Beatles' music some time before they achieved mass popularity, on a live bootleg tape from the Cavern Club which he had heard through friends working at ABC studios, near Manchester. More importantly for the Beatles, he had worked with their favourite comedians, the Goons, on a number of television and film projects. The Beatles greatly admired the surreal and anarchic humour of the Goons, and in the BBC series on sixties British cinema, *Hollywood UK*, Shenson revealed that the main reason the Beatles had accepted Lester as the film's director was that he had worked with the comedy group on various projects.[10] Their most notable film collaboration was *The Running, Jumping, and Standing Still Film* (1959), an eleven-minute short which essentially joined one of Peter Sellers' home movies with semi-improvised footage shot by Lester in less than one and a half days.

Having hired the director, Shenson needed a screenwriter. Although a number of screenplays were submitted for the project, none was considered appropriate. At the suggestion of Lester, Shenson hired Alun Owen, a scriptwriter whose previous television credits included *Z Cars* and *No Trams to Lime Street*. Like Lester, Owen was well suited to both the film-makers and its stars. He had already worked with Lester on the comedy pilot 'Dick Lester Show', and was, in the words of Alexander Walker, already a 'persona grata with the Beatles',[11] having had a similar upbringing in Merseyside. As Joe McGrath, who contributed some script ideas to the film, remembers, 'He knew where those boys were, as they say in America, coming from.'[12] Shenson briefed Owen that the script should be an 'exaggerated "day in the life"'[13] of the group and on 7 November 1963 sent Owen to Dublin to observe the Beatles' chaotic touring routine. By spring 1964 Owen's script was complete and the Beatles, on their triumphant return from America, were the most famous entertainers on earth. However, this did not affect the film's production schedule or budget, and despite the fact that the group's enormous bankability could easily have justified far greater production costs, it was decided by all parties not to drastically alter any existing agreements. However, a three-picture agreement was drawn up between United Artists and Epstein (with increasingly lucrative terms for the Beatles), and the group's profit percentage was raised. According to Lester, there was no need to increase the production budget, since they 'had the money enough' to make the kind of film they had agreed upon. 'That was the price agreed and that was it.'[14]

On 25 February, just two days after their return from America (and just six days before the start of shooting), the Beatles returned to Abbey Road to begin recording the songs which would comprise the soundtrack of the film: 'Can't Buy Me Love', 'Tell Me Why', 'If I Fell', 'You Can't Do That', 'I Should Have Known Better', 'I'm Happy Just to Dance with You', and 'And I Love Her'. However, there were some changes made to this line up. 'You Can't Do That' was dropped from the film, and the opening title song, 'A Hard Day's Night', was recorded some weeks later, in April, shortly before the completion of shooting. This song was added because the film lacked an original title and on hearing the phrase (initially a 'Ringoism') in a conversation with Lennon, Shenson decided that it perfectly captured the film's 'feel' and immediately instructed Lennon and McCartney to write the film's title song around it. Although this was the first time the group had been asked to write in a lyrically contrived manner (Shenson had given no lyrical or thematic guidelines for the other songs on the soundtrack), Lennon wrote the song in one evening and played it to the producer the following day.

In keeping with the film's modest budget, the production schedule was extremely tight, with shooting taking place at various London locations and at Twickenham studios over an eight-week period. The decision to shoot at real locations created nightmarish logistical problems for Denis O'Dell, the film's associate producer. Having arranged for British Railways to provide a special route for the Beatles' train, O'Dell discovered that information would leak out to fans who would then attempt to besiege the train. As he remembers, 'Kids would be jumping in front of the bloody train, so everyday we would change the route because we couldn't get the Beatles on the train, never mind get to shoot.'[15] For the Beatles, the speed of the shoot created a back-breaking workload. Whilst shooting the film they also had to keep abreast of a number of other commitments, including completing the soundtrack album, attending a number of awards ceremonies, and making several appearances on British television. As Mark Lewisohn's *Complete Beatles Chronicle* testifies, March to April 1964 was possibly the most chaotic period of the Beatles' career, the group sometimes moving from film locations and studios to television or recording studios in a single day.[16] Moreover, so tight was the Beatles' schedule that, at one point, (23 April) Lester was forced to shoot parts of a group sequence without Lennon, who was otherwise engaged at a literary luncheon.

Yet despite the speed and frugality of its production *A Hard Day's Night* remains, for many writers and film critics, the most accomplished and important pop musical in film history. It was described by Andrew Sarris as the '*Citizen Kane* of juke box movies'[17] and American critic Roger Ebert has commented that he would have no hesitation in placing it in the top five musicals of all time.[18] Twenty-three years after its release, a poll conducted by *Beatles Monthly Book* revealed it to be the most popular film release amongst fans, polling twice as many votes as *Help!*, the runner-up.[19] While it is not my intention to enter into puerile debate about what should constitute a film's 'classic' status, it seems that the underlying reason for the film's critical reverence rests with the originality and complexity of its formal, generic and ideological properties, properties which were conspicuously absent from previous pop films. With *A Hard Day's Night*, the pop musical 'came of age', making the vehicles of Cliff Richard and Elvis Presley seem, like their music, to be hopelessly naive and outdated.

The formal style of the film was vastly different from that of the Beatles' contemporaries, both in its extraordinary eclecticism and in its daring rejection of traditional Hollywood aesthetics. Unlike the vehicles of Tommy Steele and the later musicals of Cliff Richard, *A Hard Day's Night* was not hell-bent on merely imitating the conventional narrative structure and film style of the Hollywood musical. Instead it opted for a reactionary and seemingly self-conscious amalgamation of formal techniques derived from a range of British and European genres. What then were these techniques, from which genres were they derived, and how did they fit into the overall structure of the narrative?

Perhaps the most striking formal difference between the film and its predecessors is its illusion of documentary-style realism, which is achieved in a number of ways. From the outset, the notion of producing a film based on real characters set within (for the Beatles) realistic situations goes against the artificiality of, say, the Elvis cycle, in which Presley plays fictitious characters in overtly contrived scenarios. Although clearly 'acting', the group effectively play themselves in a narrative which, despite its fictionalized plot, accurately depicts a slice of their chaotic routine at the height of Beatlemania. As Owen stated in an interview with Alexander Walker, 'What Shenson and I want to avoid is a "slick" movie; a rough-cast look is the aim, a documentary feel. This may seem apostasy but I want a film that can stand on its own without the Beatles.'[20]

In keeping with this realist aesthetic are many of Lester's formal techniques, which are culled from a number of different realist genres, most notably drama-documentary and 'direct cinema' documentary. Indeed, despite his use of breakneck editing (possibly derived from his advertising background), the regular use of real locations, hand-held sequences and naturalistic lighting frequently imbue the action with a sense of overpowering actuality which, at times, becomes so stylistically similar to documentary or newsreel footage that it becomes impossible to differentiate fact from fiction. The opening 'chase' sequence, for example, is, although dramatized, formally consistent with contemporary direct cinema, its grainy black-and-white transparency and hand-held camerawork making it almost indistinguishable from the Maysles Brothers' documentary film of the group in America, *Yeah, Yeah, Yeah* (1964).[21] In a similar manner, Owen's script, based on direct observation and populated by Spoonerisms, colloquialisms and Liverpool slang, lends the action such a unique sense of naturalism that it also creates a convincing illusion of actuality (or at least improvisation), despite the fact that only a minimal number of genuinely 'ad-libbed' lines were employed in the final cut. Asked about the number of improvisations, cast member Victor Spinetti remembers that 'there were a hell of a lot, but they were all cut out. We kept to the script. They [the Beatles] didn't!'[22]

While realism had, of course, already been absorbed into commercial British film style through New Wave 'kitchen sink' dramas such as *A Kind of Loving* (1962) and *This Sporting Life* (1963), *A Hard Day's Night* was undoubtedly the first pop musical to adopt this aesthetic so freely and wholeheartedly into its discourse. The self-conscious integration of such realist devices might alone be enough to lend the film a sense of 'originality' and thus attract a measure of critical reverence. But what gives *A Hard Day's Night* its enduring freshness is that it is ultimately a cinematic bastard, born of a number of different and often aesthetically opposing sensibilities, skilfully pulled together by its creators into a seamless 'whole'. Quite apart from its documentary elements, the formal style of the narrative is, by the director's own admission, heavily influenced by the French *nouvelle vague*.[23] Lester's fondness for hand-held sequences and real locations are properties which can also be attributed to films such as Godard's *A Bout de Souffle* (1959), and the film's meandering narrative style seems heavily imbued with a New Wave sensibility. Although it would be misleading to suggest that the film completely lacks a classically motivated cause-effect chain (the slight story revolves around Lennon, Harrison and McCartney finding their missing drummer and getting back to the television studio in time to record their live show), the narrative embraces sequences which do nothing to advance the plot, and the group often seems merely to 'exist' within a series of episodic situations rather than to act as highly motivated, goal-oriented protagonists. Indeed, while it would be unfair to suggest that the Beatles are presented as unmotivated, it is certainly true that, like the heroes of an early Godard or Truffaut movie, they often tend to 'drift aimlessly', and 'engage in actions on the spur of the moment'.[24] The scene in which Harrison passively saunters into the production office of a patronizing fashion hipster (played by Kenneth Haigh and allegedly based on magazine editor Marc Boxer[25]) illustrates this perfectly, his conversation with the fashion boss serving no narrative purpose whatsoever. I shall discuss later the purpose that it *does* serve, but it is important to note here that Lester and Owen's narrative construction and pacing is, in effect (if not intention), closer to that of the French New Wave than to any previous British or American pop musical.

However, while there is no mistaking Lester's employment of distinctly eclectic realist techniques, the viewer's ability to perceive the action through a singularly realist aesthetic is constantly destabilized by the invasion of humorous surreal sequences and 'moments' which constantly, yet unexpectedly, hijack the illusion of actuality and 'surprise' the audience. For example, following their disagreement with a haughty bureaucrat in the train compartment, the Beatles inexplicably appear *outside* the moving train, pulling faces and taunting him with the immortal schoolboy cliché, 'Hey, Mister, can we have our ball back?' In a similar manner, the invasion of fast and slow motion action sequences, although obviously not intrinsically surrealist, imbues the text with all the gratuitous anti-logic of surrealism, and thus serves an identical aesthetic purpose. Such is the case in the park sequence (which seems highly reminiscent of Lester's own *Running, Jumping, and Standing Still Film*), where the group's antics are framed from self-consciously unconventional angles and at exaggeratedly artificial speeds. While it would be an overstatement to suggest that the use of such playful 'intrusions' into realism were original (one only has to study the early films of the French New Wave to disprove this), they were certainly new to the pop musical and, while common to the early films of Godard and Truffaut, could also have evolved from Lester's affection for the silent comedies of Buster Keaton, with whom the director was later to work. Moreover, it is possible that Lester's avant-garde sensibilities influenced some of the film's groundbreaking musical sequences, in which pop music was employed in a remarkably original capacity.

Prior to *A Hard Day's Night*, the majority of British and American pop musicals had relied upon the long established tradition of song performance derived from the classical Hollywood musical. Indeed, in the vehicles of Presley and Richard the genre's central musical sequences were based on the lip-synched performance of songs by a solo singer or group which, occasionally combined with minimal onscreen backing sources (for example, in the case of the Presley cycle, his guitar), essentially attempted to articulate the illusion of 'real' diegetic performance. While such performances were traditionally, and obviously necessarily, accompanied by non-diegetic background music (the 'unseen' musical accompaniment), the underlying importance of this formal aesthetic was to reproduce an illusory spectacle of 'genuine' performance, the key factor being the audience's belief that the stars' performances were authentic. However, Lester's partial employment of a humorous surrealism (and its resulting disposal of the conventionally 'realist' aesthetic) meant that it was no longer necessary, or, for that matter, uniformly desirable, to interpret the central musical numbers via conventionally representational sequences of performers miming to a backing track and pretending to play instruments. *A Hard Day's Night* is arguably the first film of its kind to stage central musical numbers which are not tied to performance.

While this approach is employed in the film's opening 'chase' sequence, it is also evident from the very first real musical number, 'I Should Have Known Better', where the first few verses of the song are accompanied by footage of the group playing cards in the baggage car of the train. Indeed, as with the film's non-musical sequences, Lester was keen to break with uniform performance realism as early into the film as possible in order to 'establish the principle that there would not just be realism'.[26] However, the most pronounced example of this anti-realism can be seen towards the film's closure, where 'Can't Buy Me Love' is used to accompany a sequence in which, freed from the confinements of their celebrity, the group cavort in a park. In this way, Lester's film freed the representation of the musical number from its traditional generic slavery; he allowed the pop song the opportunity to work in a similar manner to conventional incidental music, as an abstract entity capable of punctuating action which is not performance-oriented. While this move was evidently prompted by a surrealist aesthetic, it ultimately owes more to the director's need to convey the emotion inherent in the Beatles' songs; while the surrealist aesthetic made such sequences 'possible', what made them desirable was Lester's feeling that performance was not necessarily adequate to convey meaning on an emotional level. Although he accepts that the film was the first pop musical to break with performance-oriented musical numbers, the director is quick to stress that the form of the musical sequences was ultimately a by-product of a desire to convey emotion. Lester modestly explains: 'I don't think one ever sits down and says, "I'm going to do something which will change the face of musical history, and will be known in ten years' time as MTV"... You don't do it for those reasons, you do it because you think "what do you need?" [emotionally] at this point.'[27]

Even when the musical sequences *are* performance oriented, Lester ensures that they are shot with a more formally adventurous and self-consciously 'cinematic' style than had previously been seen within the genre or on such contemporaneous performance-based television shows as *Top of the Pops* (1964) or *Top Beat* (1964). Here, group-based studio performances were shot in a largely 'passive' and unpoetic manner, filmed statically from front and side (from perhaps two or three angles) and with most emphasis upon vocal performance, rather than instrumentation, as the central diegetic source. The performances in Lester's film are different. They seem deliberately to break with these conventions, and the group's musical renderings are shot from a multiplicity of angles (from above, behind, sideways and front) and camera movements, with extraordinarily fast-paced editing (which marries group footage with close-ups of screaming girls in the audience) and in a style which does not prioritize the singer above the instrumentation of the group as a whole. While such techniques differentiated the film from television aesthetics (it wouldn't have made commercial sense merely to ape television techniques), the formal experimentalism also echoes a 'playfulness' similar to the French New Wave. While it would be impossible to argue that these sequences 'liberated' pop aesthetics to the same degree as Lester's use of non-performance-based musical sequences, they did, as we will discuss in the final chapter, exert substantial influence on subsequent film and television productions.

Besides its groundbreaking form, it would also be fair to say that the film broke with a number of the ideological conventions of its genre, not least in its illusory rejection of an overtly paternalistic moral code. Where musicals such as *The Young Ones* (1961) were simple-minded morality tales in which a fictitious conflict between youth and age is resolved by mutual understanding and co-operation, *A Hard Day's Night* refused such a simplistic and contrived scenario, preferring instead to allow the audience an insight into their (albeit constructed) 'real' lives. Ultimately, it *does* promote inter-generational co-operation (the group work together to protect Paul's grandfather from danger and eventually conform to the needs of their television producer), but the film avoids the transparent moral excesses of the Cliff Richard cycle by its attachment to the illusion of realism and its resulting avoidance of stereotypical characters. While earlier films, most notably *Expresso Bongo*, had attempted to depict the inner mechanisms of the pop industry, the world which the Beatles inhabit in *A Hard Day's Night* is vastly different. The film refuses to succumb to the temptation of employing the 'conniving manager' stereotypes which peopled such movies, employing instead characters who exist outside traditional generic conventions. Indeed, while the group's manager, Norm (Norman Rossington), is presented as honest and practical (if a little bossy), Paul's trouble-stirring grandfather (Wilfred Brambell) is depicted as something of a *senile* delinquent, a self-conscious reversal of traditional stereotyping.

In this way, the film not only refuses to patronize its audience, it actually privileges it into a position of 'fly on the wall' voyeurism which, until this point, it had seldom been offered. The audience is allowed to see a pop group in intimate, 'behind-the-scenes' scenarios which are essentially 'real', or at least, realistic. In short, it works on the principle that 'truth' is more interesting (if not stranger) than 'fiction', and that the Beatles, and the newly emerging phenomenon of Beatlemania, were of greater interest to the audience than anything that could be dreamed up by a film-maker. Ultimately, it enabled the audience to leave the cinema feeling that they had come to 'know' (and love) the group as 'real' people, rather than that they had merely been 'entertained' by a pop group acting out a totally fictitious plot. The manner in which Lester and Owen fashioned the group's screen image into a presentation which was to become a turning point for both the Beatles' career and the pop film generally is worthy of further investigation.

Alexander Walker, in his book *Hollywood, England*, maintains that *A Hard Day's Night* was instrumental in altering the public's perception of the Beatles as a largely teenage phenomenon into 'the pantheon of family favourites'.[28] Although I shall later examine the validity of Walker's claim in greater detail, it would certainly be true to say that the film attempted to present audiences with a different and more complex breed of pop star than had previously been seen in Britain or America. If the film's formal cine-literacy and ideological complexity attempted to extend the genre's appeal beyond that of a teenage audience, so Owen and Lester refashioned the Beatles' image to the same end. In keeping with the film's realist aspirations, they attempted to achieve this by opting to build on the proven success of the group's pre-existing image, which had recently started to capture more mature imaginations. But what were the ingredients that constituted the pre-existing image that the film sells to its audience, and how is this achieved?

The first ingredient was humour. Even before the film was made, the group had justifiably won an international reputation for its offbeat humour and quick-witted repartee with the media, whose questions they frequently pirhana'd with a cutting yet affable humour and, at times, a simple profundity. Indeed, as Richard Buskin notes, this ingredient was vital to their conquest of America, where their unrehearsed responses to a bombardment of questions as they touched down at Kennedy Airport 'managed instantly to win the hearts of the US press and public'[29] even before they had performed any music in the country. Owen's script builds on this quality by playing on the group's comic strengths, depicting them as exaggeratedly sharp-witted characters who possess an idiosyncratic talent for acidic quipping and verbal punning. The film sets up situations in which these talents can be exploited to the full, as in the press conference sequence (possibly a reconstruction of the American conferences which took place a few weeks earlier) in which the group devise extraordinarily deft responses to the puerile questioning of the media. When asked 'How do you find America?', Lennon replies, 'Turn left at Greenland.' Asked whether he's a mod or a rocker, Ringo explains that he's a 'mocker'. In this way, the film depicts the Beatles as capable of a range of complex wit that is by turns surrealist, sardonic, sarcastic and matter-of-fact, providing 'something for everybody' regardless of humorous disposition, and exploiting an ingredient of their popularity which could not be so easily incorporated into their recordings.

The second ingredient, at least as far as British audiences were concerned, was working-class provincialism. According to Buskin, an important factor in the Beatlemania phenomenon was the fact that the group were 'four ordinary boys next door' who were 'living out a fantasy on behalf of everyone else'.[30] In a country whose popular culture had mostly been dominated by imported talent, the domestic success, let alone the international export, of any British group was a rare and welcome phenomenon. The group's unselfconscious projection of themselves as 'ordinary' and largely 'unaffected' working-class boys further endeared them to the grassroots 'underdog' sympathies of the British public and popular press, who, in their patriotic stories of the group's fame, wealth and international 'conquests', upheld them as symbols of the new social mobility and 'classlessness' of sixties Britain.[31] These sympathies were further compounded by the 'ordinariness' of the

1) The Beatles shoot a trailer for A *Hard Day's Night* at Twickenham Studios. ©Apple Corps Ltd/Walter Shenson Films.

2) George Harrison relaxes during shooting of *A Hard Day's Night.* ©Apple Corps Ltd/Walter Shenson Films.

3) Paul McCartney on the set of *A Hard Day's Night.* ©Apple Corps Ltd/Walter Shenson Films.

4) This Boy: Ringo Starr, the Beatles' 'actor'. ©Apple Corps Ltd/Walter Shenson Films.

5) A Hard Day's Night: Lennon takes five. ©Apple Corps Ltd/Walter Shenson Films.

6) Lennon on the set of *Help!* ©Apple Corps Ltd/Walter Shenson Films.

7) Harrison and McCartney perform 'I Need You'. ©Apple Corps Ltd/Walter Shenson Films.

group's provincialism (which at the time was also partly paradoxically 'exotic', since few popular acts had heralded from outside London), and the group were often presented in the press as 'just four boys from Liverpool',[32] adding fuel to the irresistible entrepreneurial fantasy that 'you don't have to be a middle-class Londoner to make it – anybody can do it.'

Like an article from a daily tabloid, the film panders to this aspect of the Beatles' successful image, portraying them as unaffected working-class boys who have 'made good' in a middle-class world through a combination of hard work and ability, whilst retaining the 'ordinariness' of their roots. Owen's script cleverly exploits this element of the Beatles' appeal, peppering their dialogue with 'hip' working-class expressions ('gear!'), colloquialisms and Liverpool slang (the expression 'grotty', which Lennon believed to have been invented by Owen, was in fact a Liverpudlian expression for 'grotesque'[33]). In some ways, this 'unashamed' presentation of working-class provincialism was very much in keeping with the new spirit of social realism which was beginning, through television dramas such as *Coronation Street* (which began in 1960) and the 'kitchen sink' films cited earlier, to become increasingly concerned with the authentic depiction of 'characters who really did breathe the essence of working-class existence'.[34] However, this is perhaps where the comparison ends. The Beatles are ultimately presented as the optimistic and successful antithesis of the angst-ridden, trapped characters of a Lindsay Anderson drama, and the world they inhabit is, by ideological necessity, almost uniformly middle-class. Nevertheless, if their presentation can largely be regarded as a factually oriented advertisement for social mobility, the group are, at times, conversely depicted as being at least partly distrustful of the environment which they inhabit, and are quick to mock the professional insincerity and transparent pretentiousness of both the middle-class television director and the professional trendsetter, whose patronizing spiel about manufacturing fashions George swiftly debunks. Moreover, the Beatles are positively presented as the antithesis of these unsavoury characters, and Owen's script plays upon the 'authenticity' and unpretentiousness of the group's 'unaffected' outlook on life. Although the film presents them as 'prisoners' of their own extraordinary celebrity, their generally affable attitude towards others is constantly shown to be unchanged by fame and wealth.

The final ingredient of the Beatles' image which Owen and Lester adapt is that of individualism. Although their famous Pierre Cardin suits and 'mop-top' haircuts symbolize and affirm a group identity, the film goes to great lengths to ensure that each Beatle is ascribed an individual personality. Indeed, although Owen could be accused of characterizing the Beatles with what Peter Brown and Steven Gaines describe as 'cartoon strokes',[35] the screenplay sometimes seems hell-bent on reassuring the audience that the Beatles are not a 'four-headed monster',[36] but a group composed of individuals with their own special character traits. As Lester explains, 'What we concentrated on was to extend, to overplay the differences in their personalities to artificially create separation.'[37]

This notion of individuality had, by 1964, already become integral to the Beatles' early success with the media, their widespread appeal deriving partly from the fact that each member appealed more strongly to different factions of their audience. Lennon and Harrison's intelligence and cynical sarcasm appealed mainly to the older, predominantly male fan, McCartney's boyish charm and more 'conventional' handsomeness to teenage girls, and Ringo's affable, goofy humour and vulnerable 'ugliness' to almost everybody else. To this end, the film allows each member an exclusive scene in which to exhibit and thus reaffirm the individual character traits which were, through television, radio and newspaper interviews, becoming a hallmark of the Beatles' media image: Ringo has his solo spot as he wanders sadly around in nowhere-land, John deflates a misguided make-up girl on the studio stairs, and George ridicules the glib London trendsetter. Only McCartney misses out on a solo scene, although this was not intentional. A sequence for McCartney (involving a humorous conversation between him and a Shakespearean actress) was shot, but was later discarded. However, the reason for its absence was not, as some writers have maintained, McCartney's performance. As Lester remembers, 'The scene looked lovely ... and there was nothing wrong with it. The general impression was that Paul couldn't do it because he didn't act it very well. That wasn't the case. What it was is by definition a very languid and gentle scene and there was no place for it when we put the film together.'[38]

Although care was taken to present the group as four individuals, it was also recognized by the film's creators that it was important for the group's female following that the Beatles should not be perceived as being romantically involved. At the heart of the female hysteria which the monster of Beatlemania fed upon was the fantasy that the 'boys-next-door' were 'available' and eligible bachelors, and A Hard Day's Night avoided wrecking the myth. As Lester maintains, 'It was an instinctive thing that fans would be quite happy with them as four available people as opposed to, I suppose, the Elvis Presley pictures, where there was always a love interest.'[39]

In line with the notion of individualism is Lester's presentation of the musical performance sequences which, as well as showcasing the group's established musical versatility (Latin ballads such as 'And I Love Her' are set against rock and roll numbers such as 'Can't Buy Me Love'), democratically allow each member of the group the opportunity to display his vocal ability. The group's major vocalists (Lennon, Harrison and McCartney) are all seen performing numbers on which they take the lead vocal. Although Harrison gets only one vocal performance ('I'm Happy Just to Dance with You'), this strategy is in keeping with the Beatles' previous two British albums, Please Please Me (1963) and With the Beatles (1963), where he is allotted one and two vocal slots respectively. The one inconsistency is the absence of a Ringo Starr vocal, although this is to some degree offset by the fact that 'I Wanna Be Your Man', a popular track from the group's previous album,[40] is heard in the disco sequence at the nightclub. Indeed, while the film employs seven new songs, a number of older Beatles numbers are used on the soundtrack. These are the aforementioned Ringo song, Harrison's 'Don't Bother Me', 'She Loves You', their biggest contemporary hit, and an orchestral rendition of a hitherto obscure Beatles B-side, 'This Boy', arranged and performed by the George Martin Orchestra and employed as incidental music. The inclusion of this material both supports the film's tendency to build on the group's existing popularity (relieving the audience of having to accustom itself to totally new material) and allows the film to work as an advertisement for other Beatles releases as well as the official soundtrack album.

With shooting completed by the end of April 1964, the film received an intensive publicity campaign from United Artists, and under Lester's supervision a series of trailers were produced which, in the case of the European version, featured an exclusive appearance from the group absurdly addressing audiences from prams! However, despite territorial variations, the central marketing theme of both trailers and publicity posters was, unsurprisingly, the group's music, and both British and American publicity proudly announced the forthcoming appearance of the seven new songs and included advertisements for the soundtrack album, whose cover cleverly used the same typography as the film posters, creating a kind of corporate 'package'. The company also went to great lengths to ensure that the film received high-profile openings, particularly in America, where they organized free buses, food and security for fan-club members to generate media interest by camping outside the doors of the cinema the night before the premiere. In Britain, the film's release was even more of a 'media event'. On 6 July the film was given a Royal Charity Premiere (in the presence of Princess Margaret) at the London Pavilion in Piccadilly Circus. Twelve thousand Beatles fans turned up in the hope of catching a glimpse of their idols as they entered the cinema. These events garnered enormous publicity for the Beatles, and the tabloid papers ran cover and centre-page stories on the film's opening with headlines such as 'A Royal Shake for Ringo' and 'It's a Right Royal Riot of a Film'.[41] The Beatles were, of course, already big celebrities in Britain, but the photographs depicting the group shaking hands with Princess Margaret added an extra dimension of exoticism to their image. More importantly, they consolidated the royal 'seal of approval' which had initially been triggered by the Beatles' Royal Command performance in 1963, making them the first pop group to win the public approval of 'establishment' figures.

If the publicity which surrounded the film made the Beatles' star shine even brighter, this was matched by the effect of the film itself. It garnered almost unanimously favourable reviews in both the broadsheet and tabloid press, with the highest praise coming from *Daily Mirror* critic Dick Richards, who stated that 'what could have been simply a money-making gimmick turns out as nimble entertainment in its own right. It's offbeat – and on the beat. It's a winner.'[42] Film journals such as *Sight and Sound*, although slightly less generous, maintained, perhaps somewhat grudgingly, that the film 'works … on a level at which most British films, particularly the bigger and more pretentious, don't manage to get going at all.'[43] Furthermore, the film's positive critical reception was not restricted to the press, and both George Martin and Alun Owen won Academy Award nominations for their efforts with soundtrack and script.

With the combination of fever-pitch Beatlemania and favourable reviews, a film which was initially financed for soundtrack material became an enormous international box-office success in its own right, taking $1.3 million in its first week of American release, and eventually grossing $11 million worldwide.[44] Needless to say, the accompanying soundtrack material also sold extraordinarily well, the British album retaining a number one position for twenty-one weeks and the title-track single for three weeks. A tie-in novelization of Owen's screenplay (complete with eight pages of stills from the film) by John Burke also sold well on both sides of the Atlantic. The profits didn't stop there. Three years later, the film was sold to the American television network, NBC, for £1.5 million,[45] a very considerable figure for the sixties.

The film's success affected the Beatles' career in a number of significant ways. First, it helped to consolidate their appeal to a teenage audience. Conversely, however, it also helped to develop and expand their appeal beyond that of contemporary youth and there were a number of factors which contributed to this. The form and ideology of the film appealed more to the aesthetic tastes of an adult audience than any previous pop movie. Fortunately for the Beatles, this was recognized by the media, and while the royal associations of the premiere helped to consolidate and 'legitimize' the group's appeal to a more middle-aged audience, positive reviews in such 'highbrow' papers as the *Sunday Times* and the *Daily Telegraph* also helped to boost their cultural credibility with more middle-class and intellectual factions than they had previously been afforded, winning over remaining 'non-believers'.[46] While this kind of 'intellectual' media treatment wasn't totally new to the Beatles as a recording outfit (a year earlier the *Sunday Times* had declared Lennon and McCartney the 'outstanding English composers of 1963' and compared their chord progressions to the music of Mahler[47]), the film and its criticism also helped to transform them from a 'faceless' recording group into an act which comprised four separate 'personalities'. This was particularly true of American audiences and, as Roger Ebert claims, 'After that movie was released everybody knew the names of all four Beatles ... everybody.'[48] In short, the crossover into film helped to furnish the Beatles with a total mass appeal hitherto unprecedented in pop. Moreover, this had been achieved without sacrificing a shred of credibility within the ranks of their original audience, a rare feat indeed.

On a more personal level, the film marked the beginning of a longstanding professional friendship with Victor Spinetti, who was to go on to appear in the group's next two film projects, and to co-adapt Lennon's books, *In His Own Write* (1964) and *A Spaniard in the Works* (1965), for the stage in 1968. As he recalls, 'When we met it was as if we'd known each other all of our lives, it was just one of those things... There was no sort of a wall ... I just loved them.'[49] The film also provided the location for George Harrison's first meeting with Patti Boyd, who was working as a bit-part actress (she can be seen playing a schoolgirl in the train sequences). Harrison went on to marry Boyd in early 1966, and although they later divorced (Boyd married Harrison's guitarist friend Eric Clapton in the seventies), she was responsible for introducing Harrison to the teachings of Maharishi Mahesh Yogi, the guru whose philosophies became of vital importance to the Beatles' own ideas in 1967/68.

Despite the critical and economic success of *A Hard Day's Night*, the Beatles remained impassive about their film career, and were modest about their abilities as actors. Shortly after the film was released Lennon was asked if the public could look forward to more Beatles movies. 'There'll be more,' came the reply, 'but I don't know whether you can look forward to them or not.'[50]

Notes

1. 'Beatlemania!,' *Daily Mirror*, 2 November 1963. The paper coined the term in a report following a concert in Cheltenham.
2. For a fascinating overview of early pop movies see Doggett, 1995, pp. 46–9.
3. Lewisohn, 1992, p. 145. According to Lewisohn, the show, broadcast at 8 p.m. on Sunday 9 February 1964, resulted in viewing figures of seventy-three million, then the biggest audience for any programme on American television.
4. A more detailed discussion of United Artists' interest in capitalizing on the potential of the soundtrack material can be seen in the documentary home video release *You Can't Do That: the Making of A Hard Day's Night* (VCI, 1994).
5. Ibid.
6. Barrow, 1993a, p. 5.
7. Ibid., p. 5.
8. Percentage and Beatles' fee from Walker, 1986, p. 232. Budget figure from Dick Lester, interviewed by author, 26 March 1996. It should be noted, however, that due to careful planning and a number of skilfully executed publicity deals by Denis O'Dell, the film actually came in around £20,000 under budget.
9. Barrow, 1993a, p. 7.
10. *Hollywood UK*, BBC, broadcast September 1993.

11. Walker, 1986, p. 237.
12. Joe McGrath, interviewed by author, 13 February 1996.
13. *You Can't Do That: the Making of A Hard Day's Night* (VCI, 1994)
14. Dick Lester, interviewed by author, 26 March 1996.
15. Denis O'Dell, interviewed by author, 30 April 1996.
16. See Lewisohn, 1992, pp. 184–92.
17. *You Can't Do That: the Making of A Hard Day's Night* (VCI, 1994).
18. Ibid.
19. 'Poll Results', *Beatles Monthly Book*, no. 134, June 1987, pp. 19–21. Interestingly, the soundtrack album also achieves a respectable position, number 6 in the album listings.
20. Walker, 1986, p. 238.
21. This Maysles Brothers' documentary was networked in Britain on 12 February 1964 by Granada, and in America (in a slightly different version and with the title of *What's Happening! the Beatles in the USA*) in November 1964.
22. Victor Spinetti, interviewed by author, 29 April 1996.
23. In *You Can't Do That: the Making of A Hard Day's Night* (VCI, 1994), Lester maintains that he attempted to combine the best elements of the *nouvelle vague* with an 'earthy Englishness'.
24. Bordwell and Thompson, 1979, p. 321.
25. Joe McGrath, interviewed by author. McGrath maintains that Owen based the character on Boxer. Lester believes this to be 'vaguely' correct, maintaining that 'it was Alun Owen's idea', although he is uncertain whether Owen actually knew Boxer. To the best of my knowledge, Owen never commented.
26. Dick Lester, interviewed by author.
27. Ibid.
28. Walker, 1986, p. 242.
29. Buskin, 1994, p. 12.
30. Ibid., pp. 10–11.
31. An illuminating discussion of class and social mobility in the sixties can be found in Wheen, 1982. Here, the author discusses the so-called 'classlessness' of the decade as something of a superficial facade perpetrated by the British media's lionization of working-class entertainers and celebrities.
32. Interestingly, this approach was also absorbed into literature, and the back cover of the group's only official biography, *The Beatles* (Davies, 1969), describes the group as 'four working-class Liverpool lads who in four years became millionaires and the best known people in the world'.
33. Lennon's misunderstanding is documented in Miles, 1978, p. 107. Owen sets the record straight in the documentary, *You Can't Do That: the Making of A Hard Day's Night* (VCI, 1994).
34. Marwick, 1990, p. 134.
35. Brown and Gaines, 1984, p. 116.
36. Walker, 1986, p. 239.
37. Dick Lester, interviewed by author.
38. Ibid.
39. Ibid.
40. The huge popularity of the song derived from the fact that it had also been recorded by the Rolling Stones and released as a single the previous year.
41. *Daily Mirror*, 7 July 1964.
42. Dick Richards, 'It's a Right Royal Riot of a Film', *Daily Mirror*, 7 July 1964.
43. Geoffrey Nowell-Smith, *Sight and Sound*, vol. 33, no. 4, 1964, p. 197.
44. First figure from Buskin, 1994, p. 10. Second from Walker, 1986, p. 241. Walker's figure dates from mid-1971.

45. Figure taken from Barrow, 1993a, p. 11.

46. See reviews by Dilys Powell, *Sunday Times*, 12 July 1964, and Patrick Gibb, 'Much to Enjoy in A Hard Day's Night', *Daily Telegraph*, 7 July 1964. Powell maintains that the film is a 'sharply professional piece', while Gibb describes the Beatles performances as 'engagingly provocative.'

47. William Mann, review of *With the Beatles* LP, *The Times*, 23 December 1963.

48. *You Can't Do That: the Making of A Hard Day's Night* (VCI, 1994).

49. Victor Spinetti, interviewed by author.

50. Barrow, 1993a, p. 11.

2

Acting Naturally?
Help!

After the success of *A Hard Day's Night*, the Beatles went back to the recording studio to work on their next album, *Beatles for Sale* (1964). Although retrospectively condemned as somewhat lacklustre by the majority of critics,[1] the album also sold very respectably, replacing *A Hard Day's Night* at the top of the British album charts and enjoying an intermittent run of eleven weeks in that position. By the Beatles' standards, 1965 began fairly uneventfully and, after completing their run of Christmas shows at the Hammersmith Odeon, the group took a well-earned break before returning to Abbey Road to begin work on the soundtrack of the second film for United Artists, provisionally titled *Beatles 2*. This title was later to change to *Eight Arms to Hold You* (another 'Ringoism'), and would eventually become *Help!*

Unlike their first film, the colour-shot *Help!* was a lavish affair, the success of *A Hard Day's Night* no doubt convincing the producers and financiers that an inflated budget and a less intense shooting schedule could be justified in the light of the Beatles' ever-increasing popularity. According to Alexander Walker's figures, the film was budgeted at £400,000,[2] twice the cost of their previous production, and the shooting schedule, which spanned eleven weeks (between 23 February and 11 May), was almost one third longer than that of *A Hard Day's Night*. Again the same successful combination of Lester and Shenson were employed as director and producer, although the screenplay was written by Marc Behm and Charles Wood rather than Alun Owen, whose script had been integral to the success of *A Hard Day's Night*. It is possible that the Beatles were at least partly responsible for this decision, as records show that the relationship between them and Owen was characterized by a mutual, although mild, dislike. In a 1993 interview, Owen stated that he 'didn't really get on with John Lennon',[3] and as Tony Barrow revealed some years earlier, the Beatles 'tolerated rather than enjoyed their relationship with Alun Owen'.[4] Lennon was particularly uncharitable about Owen's personality, and some years after the film was made described him as 'a bit phoney, like a professional Liverpool man – you know, like a professional American'.[5]

Despite the fact that *Help!* was essentially the construction of the same team, the narrative premises of the two films differ enormously. Unlike the realist-oriented aesthetic of *A Hard Day's Night*, *Help!* was conceived as pure fiction fantasy, and while it retains the notion of the Beatles 'as themselves', the writers had no intention of attempting to construct an illusion of actuality. Instead, they created a totally fictitious extravaganza in which the Beatles are pursued across various exotic locations by an assortment of mad scientists, Eastern mystics and bumbling policemen who want to get hold of the highly prized diamond ring, Kaili, which has inexplicably become stuck to Ringo's finger.

The final synopsis of the filmed screenplay has a fascinating and complex history, made all the more difficult to fathom by the conflicting memories of those concerned. However, it would appear that the origins of the underlying 'chase' premise of the final script evolved from an original treatment, which had to be jettisoned for external reasons. The original treatment was written, to greater or lesser degrees, by Dick Lester and Joe McGrath, who by 1965 had also been involved with the Beatles in a number of ways, having produced and directed such television shows as *A Degree of Frost* and *Not Only But Also* (in which members of the group had appeared), as well as contributing some script ideas to *A Hard Day's Night*. Because of the conflicting recollections of McGrath and Lester, there are some minor differences over both the extent of authorship and the plot of the original synopsis. Lester maintains that the outline was an 'idea of mine'[6] which he talked through with McGrath, and McGrath maintains that he was 'paid a lot of money'[7] by Shenson to produce the treatment. However, since the stories they recount are essentially very similar, and both directors were, in Lester's terms, 'very good friends' and would 'always talk up ideas',[8] it is not unreasonable to suppose that they collaborated on the original rejected treatment.

As Joe McGrath remembers it, the original synopsis of the Beatles' second film was 'based on a very old film idea':[9] Ringo is told by a doctor that he is terminally ill and becomes so depressed that he immediately pays a contract killer £500 to dispose of him. Unable to face immediate termination, he asks the killer to destroy him when he least expects it. This should be easy, since the killer is also a master of disguise. However, the following day the doctor phones and confesses that he has made a terrible mistake, telling Ringo that the X-rays used to diagnose the drummer's illness belonged to somebody else and that he is not terminally ill at all. Unfortunately Ringo, unable to trace the master of disguise, panics and tells the other Beatles of his predicament. With this premise established, there follows a series of comic chases and mishaps in which the Beatles attempt to trace the killer before he can carry out his task. However, Lester remembers things slightly differently. As he recalls it, Ringo's motivation for hiring the hit man was that he is tired of the constraints of his fame, and in a drunken stupor meets a man in a pub who then hires the killer. The following morning a sober Ringo regrets his actions and, as with the other recollection, there then ensues a series of comic chases and scrapes in which the Beatles attempt to track down the master of disguise before he can terminate their drummer's life.

According to Lester, the idea, which he had already talked through with Paul McCartney, had to be jettisoned because a similar screenplay was, by 'pure accident'[10] already being shot in Hong Kong as *Chinese Adventures in China* by Philippe de Broca (aka *Up to His Ears*). However, he liked the premise and approached American writer Marc Behm with a view to producing a similar story. 'Out of that,' recalls Lester, 'came the fact that Ringo, for one reason or another, was being attacked by people and didn't understand why…'[11] Once this synopsis was written by Behm, Lester then drafted in Charles Wood (who had written *The Knack*) to give the story the English context which, as an American living in Paris, was beyond Behm's experience. As Lester remembers, Behm's story had 'no English context at all, so Charles came in and we rewrote it to suit them [the Beatles] and the Englishness of it all.'[12]

Like the original treatment, the film's title also faced considerable technical problems. From the outset, Lester had wanted to use the title *Help, Help* but was initially unable to use it because it had already been registered in America. As a result, the shooting title went through a number of changes until well into filming, when it was decided that the then current title, *Eight Arms to Hold You* was both disliked and unsuitable as the basis for the as yet unwritten title song. Lester then went to United Artists' lawyers and asked, 'What is the law? Can you copyright the word "Help"? ... OK, somebody else has registered it but it's like saying that somebody's registered the word "and" ... Shakespeare used the word "and", so we can't use it?'[13] After he had decided to go ahead and use the title anyway, one of the lawyers told Lester that the registered title did not have an exclamation point, so one was added as 'a legal wheeze'[14] to avoid potential problems.

Whatever the truth about the authorship of the original script and its eventual rejection, there can be no doubt about the fundamental change of direction which the move into pure fiction heralded. For all its silent movie surrealism, Lester's first Beatles film had concentrated on artificially creating an appearance of genuine actuality, on convincing audiences that what they were perceiving on screen was an authentic slice of the group's life. In essence, what he presented was a film 'about' the Beatles. With *Help!* that changed. He was now making a film 'starring' the Beatles. Considering the enormous success of *A Hard Day's Night*, the decision to move into pure fiction initially seems somewhat perplexing and, before I discuss the film in detail, I want to posit some theories as to why the Beatles and the film's producers decided to break with a formula which had thus far served them so well.

This is a complex issue, and the problem is compounded by the fact that the Beatles have never discussed the matter in any great detail. Any suggestions I make are therefore inevitably speculative. However, I believe the move to have been affected by a number of contributory factors. First, and perhaps most obviously, the film-makers had the money to do it. While I am certainly not suggesting that the first film was made with a documentary aesthetic simply because the team had a more modest budget, it is reasonable to suggest that the budget of *Help!* befitted a more lavish style of film-making than the previous movie, and that this allowed them to make a far more convincing and elaborate fantasy film than would have ever been possible in previous circumstances.

On a broader level, it must also be noted that the emphasis upon different forms of realism was, by 1965, beginning to wane. In particular, the British social realism of 'kitchen sink' films such as *Room at the Top* (1959), *Saturday Night and Sunday Morning* (1960), *A Taste of Honey* (1961) and *A Kind of Loving* (1962) was giving way to the fiction of the spy cycles of James Bond and Harry Palmer, the ever popular *Carry On* series, and 'swinging' sex comedies such as Lester's own *The Knack* (1965), which he shot between his two Beatles movies. Increasing American investment in more lavish British productions, coupled with a new sense of national affluence and optimism, had conspired against the 'angry young men', and the black-and-white Northern provincialism of the early sixties was gradually superseded by colour films which were increasingly London-based, lighthearted, and 'international' in both style and subject matter.

There were, however, other possible reasons why it was inadvisable to make another realist-oriented film. The Beatles were now living out a reality which would have contrasted too greatly with the clean-cut image upon which their popularity had until now depended. Introduced to the pleasures of smoking marijuana in 1964 by Bob Dylan,[15] they were soon frequent users of the drug, and by early 1965 and the shooting of *Help!* they were, in Lester's words, 'stoned a bit too much and they kept losing the script. There were a lot of sequences where I'd be off-camera saying the line to them and they'd say the line back to me.'[16] As the director explained in the BBC's *Hollywood UK* television series, 'The documentary style of *A Hard Day's Night* was no longer appropriate or even possible since by that time the Beatles were world celebrities living X-rated lives, and no longer able to appear as the lads from Liverpool.'[17] Moreover, the idea of making a fiction film probably appealed to the group because it allowed them to escape from participating in a movie which would, by implication, inevitably have to deal intensively with the concept of Beatlemania, a subject which was becoming increasingly unbearable for the group.

By 1965, the novelty of their stardom was beginning to wear thin, and they had become increasingly disillusioned by the personal restrictions which came with international adoration and which had been so lightheartedly treated by *A Hard Day's Night*. Commenting some years later on Beatlemania, Lennon maintained that 'all that business was awful. It was a fucking humiliation. One has to completely humiliate oneself to be what the Beatles were, and that's what I resent.'[18] Indeed, if they could ill afford to expose the realities of their 'X-rated lives' to the public, then this was matched by their unwillingness so to do. For the Beatles, having to laugh and joke their way through a film in the same vein as *A Hard Day's Night* would have probably seemed like a very sick joke. So it is quite possible that the initial impetus for making a totally fictitious film was partly instigated by the Beatles' own need to escape from the imprisonment of Beatlemania and to find themselves a scenario which was constructed 'around' rather than 'about' them, and a plot-driven film which neither they, nor their phenomenon, would have to 'carry' to anything like the same degree as before. Although they were playing a loose amalgamation of 'themselves' again, the plot-driven script and fantastical scenario allowed them to approach acting without the levels of self-consciousness and trepidation demanded by the authenticity of Owen's semi-realist screenplay, thus allowing them to become, in Lester's word, 'passengers'[19] in their own film, a notion which by 1965 they were probably keen to accept.

More importantly for the increasingly powerful yet world-weary Beatles, the film's lighthearted premise enabled them to use their fame to their own advantage and to make requests of the writers and producers which would, by conventional film-making standards, be considered ludicrous. Indeed, some years later McCartney revealed that the scenes shot in Austria and the Bahamas were contrived by the writers at the group's request simply because they were places they wanted to visit. As McCartney puts it, 'I remember one of the first conversations was, hey, can't we go somewhere sunny? … The Bahamas? Sure, we could write a scene in where you go to the Bahamas. And ski-ing? We'd like to go ski-ing! It was like ordering up your holidays.'[20] While some writers have alleged that the Bahamas locations were chosen purely for tax evasion purposes,[21] it is clearly likely that, for the Beatles at least, the move into fiction was above all a tonic which, in the spirit of democratic compromise, allowed the group to escape the rigours of Beatlemania whilst simultaneously stoking its flames. As McCartney commented some time later, ' … that was what we were trying to do, get on with our lives but at the same time make a film.'[22]

Another possible influence on the move to fiction was the fact that the success of *A Hard Day's Night* had triggered a host of imitation vehicles for British stars such as Gerry and the Pacemakers, Herman's Hermits and the Dave Clark Five. As Peter Noone commented, 'Herman's Hermits' first movie was basically a pure copy of that genre... Everybody was making one.'[23] Although Lester has said that this was not necessarily a major factor in the move, few could deny that it was theoretically prudent of the Beatles' camp to avoid falling into a style which, by 1965, was fast becoming a cliché. While falling into such a cliché might well have been acceptable for some, dare we say, 'lesser' artists, such an approach was hardly in keeping with the Beatles' style. After all, their previous musical and cinematic success had seemed, at least in part, to stem from their willingness to stay 'one step ahead of the game'. Indeed, while their previous film had broken with the array of conventions discussed in the previous chapter, the success of their musical career had also partly stemmed from their being the first pop group to write their own material and to arrange it with unparalleled versatility. By 1965 it was clear that audiences and critics not only wanted the group's product to develop and change, they expected it, and anything less than a new direction would be intolerable. But what kind of 'new direction' were the Beatles taking and, more precisely, what kind of fiction film did *Help!* turn out to be?

The most popular British film of 1962 was the United Artists feature, *Dr No.* Its success was consolidated a year later by *From Russia with Love*, and in 1964 by the enormously popular *Goldfinger*. The Bond cycle was the biggest cinematic attraction in Britain and, by 1965 and the making of *Help!*, it seemed there to stay. Although clearly not conceived from the outset as a Bond parody or pastiche, *Help!*'s finished screenplay manages to mine the popularity of the Bond films in a number of ways. First, the subject matter and narrative construction of the film seem highly reminiscent of the Bond cycle and, although Lester maintains that the Bond connection is limited to a number of inconsequential jokes (he holds that 'you could take all the Bond references out and the film would remain the same'[24]), I would argue that Behm and Wood's screenplay includes many quintessentially 'Bondesque' ingredients.

The most obvious pastiche of the Bond cycle is the story itself, which, like the then recent *Goldfinger*, involves a spy-oriented chase through similar exotic locations, the Beatles film substituting Austria for Switzerland. Moreover, the film employs many sequences which were fast becoming staple ingredients of the Bond cycle, including a set-piece fist fight (where the Beatles are attacked by a group of Clang's henchmen) and a car chase sequence (of sorts) in which Ringo, dumped in the boot of Professor Foot's car, is freed by George after he heroically commandeers the vehicle by making it spin off the road. Furthermore, there are close similarities between the two films' opening credit sequences. Like *Goldfinger*, *Help!* employs an elaborate opening credit song (a slightly tinted black-and-white sequence in which the Beatles, projected onto a white screen in Clang's lair, perform the title track while he throws darts at them), its entrance delayed by an opening scene which establishes the initial narrative equilibrium.

However, while the story seems to pastiche the subject matter and narrative construction of the Bond films, *Help!* conversely seems determined to include elements of spoofery which deliberately and self-consciously parody the Bond cycle. Indeed, although Lester feels that 'it would be dangerous' to describe such elements as parodic (he prefers the term 'pastiche,' maintaining that 'you don't parody something that is in itself a parody'[25]), I would maintain that the film's core of humour is dominated by intelligent and often hilarious parodic tendencies, and that the film gently and affectionately sends up several aspects of the Bond movies, most notably the stock characters of the 007 pictures (and particularly the stereotypical 'Bondesque' villains), who are invariably transposed into comic figures. Perhaps the most obvious example is the comic recreation of the mad scientist 'type', Professor Foot (Victor Spinetti), whose implausible inventions designed to secure him world domination consistently backfire to humorous effect. Likewise, the bumbling, accident-prone cult leader Clang (Leo McKern) is clearly imbued with 'Bond villain' character traits. Like Auric Goldfinger, he is both exotic and power-crazed, yet his attempts to recover the sacred ring of Kaili inevitably end in comic misfire. In a similar manner, the Beatles film also parodies the fickle heroine (Eleanor Bron) who, like Pussy Galore, switches sides to help the 'good guys' when she sees the error of her ways. Beyond the humorous sending-up of these stereotypes, the film also manages to poke fun at the Bond films' obsession with scientific gadgetry, and the narrative is crammed with comic scenes which ridicule the sophistication and ruthless efficiency of the hi-tech devices featured in *Goldfinger*. Indeed, the ordinary and ineffective household paint which is used to coat Ringo is clearly a humorous send-up of the deadly skin-suffocation spray used by Goldfinger, while Oddjob's equally deadly steel bowler hat is hilariously parodied by the ineffective, unfurling turban used as a weapon by Clang's henchman, Blutha (John Bluthal).

By overtly parodying and pastiching elements of the Bond films whilst also mimicking elements of their narrative construction, *Help!* manages to 'have its cake and eat it', gently poking fun at the cycle whilst simultaneously employing their formulaic properties to enhance the film's commercial appeal. In this way, *Help!* can be regarded as a precursor of a number of other similarly exploitative (although vastly inferior) Bond spoofs, such as *Our Man Flint* (1965), *In Like Flint* (1967) and the *Dr Goldfoot* series.

However, despite its fictional premise and parodic inclinations, it would also be true to say that there are several fundamental similarities between *Help!* and the group's previous film, although these are often marked by subtle yet significant developments and variations.

First, Lester's direction retains several similarities and, although it is less formally eclectic than its predecessor, he imbues the film with a similar fondness for surreal slapstick and playful formal humour which are clearly derived from his love of silent comedy. Perhaps the best example of this is his use of the unexpected surreal intrusion of title cards which, intercut with causally unrelated shots of the Beatles romping in a wood, signify 'end of part one', 'intermission', 'end of intermission', and 'part two'. Likewise, Lester shoots the Beatles walking simultaneously into four ordinary-looking terraced houses before a cut to the inside of the houses reveals that they are all part of an enormous and luxurious sixties 'pad' crammed with sunken beds, Wurlitzer organs and state-of-the-art technology.

Moreover, Lester applies the same pioneering techniques to the musical sequences as in *A Hard Day's Night*, again using pop music as an accompaniment to non-performance-oriented action. The best example of this occurs in what is arguably the film's most memorable sequence, where the Beatles' most recent single, 'Ticket to Ride', accompanies footage of the group attempting to ski down the Austrian piste. Interestingly, however, the majority of this sequence was shot in a reverse manner to the more carefully staged antics of the 'Can't Buy Me Love' scene of the previous film: the director merely instructed the group (who were totally untrained skiers) to go and play around on the slopes, and then edited the largely unchoreographed footage to fit the song in post-production. As such, the 'Ticket to Ride' sequence is arguably the first time that the full potential of editing for pace and rhythm was prioritized above choreography in a pop film. Moreover, there were other formal developments in the presentation of the musical numbers. In the sequence which accompanies McCartney's 'Another Girl', Lester presents the group's performance in a semi-diegetic manner, simultaneously combining a realist and an anti-realist approach as McCartney is shown realistically lip-synching fragments of the song's words but actually 'playing' a bikini-clad model as though she were his guitar!

Interestingly, the technique of employing semi-diegetic performance footage was shortly to become integral to the pioneering promotional clips of Joe McGrath, who on 23 November 1965 directed the group in their first ten promotional videos, which were made through Intertel and financed by the Beatles' management agency, NEMS. These promos, which featured several different versions of five Beatles songs ('We Can Work It Out', 'Daytripper', 'I Feel Fine', 'Ticket to Ride' and 'Help!'), occupy a unique position in television history for a number of reasons. They were the first independently produced pop films to be made and distributed specifically for the international market, anticipating the beginning of contemporary pop video. Moreover, while their ultimate *raison d'être* (to allow the Beatles total control over their image and to be seen simultaneously all over the world) closely mirrors that of the group's move into feature films, so too does their form. Unlike the performance-oriented construction of contemporary pop shows, several of McGrath's promos partially disposed of this notion, the most notable example being the 'I Feel Fine' clip, which features the group miming into a punch-bag while Ringo rides an exercise bicycle.

Another similarity between *Help!* and *A Hard Day's Night* is the music of the soundtrack itself, although, as we shall see, there are again subtle differences and developments within this schemata. Like *A Hard Day's Night*, the film contained a quota of seven new Beatles numbers and again showcased the impressive versatility of their songwriting. Like the previous film, the *Help!* soundtrack included folk ballads (Lennon's 'You've Got to Hide Your Love Away') upbeat rock and roll numbers (McCartney's 'The Night Before') and love songs (Harrison's 'I Need You'). In keeping with established precedent, Harrison was again allotted one solo vocal performance ('I Need You') with the remainder equally divided between Lennon and McCartney. Again, the action is accompanied by a quota of previously successful Beatles songs, including the group's own recording of 'She's a Woman' (the British and American B-side to their 1964 number one 'I Feel Fine') and another orchestral arrangement of 'A Hard Day's Night'. Moreover, like the soundtrack album to the previous film, the British and American LPs were issued in different formats. While the US release coupled the seven new Beatles tracks featured in the film with the orchestral score, the British release complemented the film songs with seven other numbers.

Despite these similarities, there are some interesting differences in the musical and lyrical content of the Beatles' film songs. Unlike the happy-go-lucky and optimistic sentiments of the *Hard Day's Night* music, the lyrics of Lennon's contributions to *Help!* boasted a more serious, confessional and mature tone. Indeed, in some ways *Help!* marks the turning point at which Lennon (perhaps under the influence of Bob Dylan, whom the Beatles greatly admired) began to abandon the notion of writing throwaway, 'boy meets girl' lyrics in favour of a more heartfelt and 'genuine' self-expression which transcended the bland love themes of old and heralded the start of a more introspective approach in the Beatles' songwriting. Indeed, the Dylanesque lyrics of 'You've Got to Hide Your Love Away', with their intricate wordplay and tone of morbid self-pity and doubt, evoked a far more complex and 'adult' emotional depth than any of the love songs which appeared in *A Hard Day's Night*. The title track, whilst 'written to order', rejected the love song format altogether, the introspective and subconsciously confessional lyric being based on its author's personal feelings of insecurity and desperation as the onslaught of Beatlemania took its toll. As Lennon himself explained, 'I was fat and depressed and I was crying out for help.'[26] Although a number of critics have maintained that Lennon's songs began to become more lyrically complex prior to the making of the *Help!* soundtrack ('I'm a Loser' from the *Beatles for Sale* album is often cited as his first 'personal' and/or self-revelatory song[27]), the title track was the first Beatles song to reject the love theme formula outright, and as such can be viewed as something of a watershed in the Beatles' recording career. As Mark Hertsgaard remarks, 'It was the first Beatles song in which the words were the point at least as much as the music.'[28] Indeed, although the song's lyrical significance went largely unnoticed by audiences (as Lennon said in 1980, 'Most people think it's just a fast rock and roll song'[29]), it was nevertheless a precursor of the introspective self-expression which was to become a trademark of their subsequent recordings.

Musically, the songs which appeared in the film also displayed a growing complexity and maturity. While evoking the same eclectic versatility as the songs from the previous film, the Beatles were expanding their musical horizons in leaps and bounds, incorporating new instruments into their arrangements (the flute solo on 'You've Got to Hide Your Love Away', Harrison's pedal steel guitar on 'I Need You') and complexifying the traditional '4/4' time signatures of rock and roll arrangements with jagged, broken offbeats which, in the case of 'Ticket to Ride', splinter and offset the traditional backbeat of old with a piercing freshness hitherto unheard in pop. Indeed, if audiences failed to consciously grasp the new lyrical direction of the Beatles' songs, it was impossible to miss the new 'feel' of the music of 'Ticket to Ride', which evoked, in Ian MacDonald's term, the most 'intense'[30] sound the group had produced for some time.

Finally, the representation of the group remained very similar to that of *A Hard Day's Night*. Indeed, all the characteristics of their former screen incarnation are intact: Lennon's cutting wit is highlighted in the sequence where the group visit Scotland Yard (asked by a detective how long he thinks the group will last, he retorts by asking the detective how long he thinks the inquiries for the 'Great Train Robbery' will last), and McCartney's boyish sex appeal is also suggested by the inviting glances he receives from Eleanor Bron. However, within this schemata there are again slight differences, the most obvious being the absence of the 'solo' scenes which characterized the narrative construction of the earlier film and which results in the viewer perceiving the group as more of a single unit than four separate and individual personalities. Indeed, because the film is plot-driven rather than character-driven, the Beatles themselves really do become passengers in a narrative which is so determined on assaulting the senses with nonstop visual slapstick, breakneck editing and formal trickery that their own characters tend to become somewhat submerged in an ocean of dazzling technique. Indeed, as one critic later commented, 'In *Help!* they are still themselves, but are caught in such a web of wild comedy they seem at times as trapped as four flies waiting for spider Lester to bring them back into the parlour.'[31]

However, while the group's individuality becomes somewhat obscured in the film, it might be fair to suggest that Ringo is offered the most opportunity to 'act' and, although his sequences are perhaps slightly less character-based than those of the first movie, the narrative again revolves more around him (as the wearer of the ring) than any of the other Beatles. Starr had received the best notices for his performance in *A Hard Day's Night*,[32] and it was natural for him, as the group's 'actor', to take a bigger role in the second film. Furthermore, it would be fair to say that of the individual characters in the group he was the one with the most all-round appeal and sympathy. As Lester maintains, 'If you're going to choose somebody to have [as a central character], he's the one that the audience has the most immediate bonding with. He was a very endearing personality.'[33] Indeed, if Lennon and Harrison's projection appealed more to male fans and McCartney's to predominantly teenage girls, Starr's naturally comic hangdog appearance and less sarcastic wit exuded an appeal which included but also transcended these factions and, as Starr has recalled, his fan-base also comprised 'the mothers and the children'.[34] Placing the most 'popular' Beatle at the centre of the narrative was therefore as shrewd a commercial move as adopting the family-oriented Bond-style story; it was a plea for mass appeal which echoed his developing musical role in the Beatles, as singer of a range of material which, as well as including teenage anthems (such as 'Boys') would comprise songs seemingly specifically tailored to suit the tastes of the mature adults or very young children who were normally considered beyond the potential radius of appeal for a pop band. Indeed, throughout his entire career as a Beatle, Ringo would be given or choose material that would mainly comprise of 'adult' country and western songs such as 'Act Naturally' and 'Honey Don't', or 'children's' nursery rhymes and lullabies such as 'Yellow Submarine' and 'Goodnight'.

With principal photography for the film completed on 11 May 1965, the release and marketing of *Help!* followed an almost identical pattern to the previous film. Again it was accompanied by the near-concurrent release of a soundtrack album, a single (the title track) and a novelization. Again it was publicized by a Royal premiere at the London Pavilion (29 July). Again this was attended by Princess Margaret, and again the event attracted around 10,000 fans to Piccadilly Circus. Moreover, the promotional posters for the film were almost a blueprint of the first movie's, with the pop art lettering emphasizing the major selling point of seven brand-new songs.

However, if the release and marketing slants of the films were identical, then the reviews weren't. *Help!* elicited a mixed bag of critical reactions, ranging from extravagant praise to harsh criticism. Indeed, while *Sunday Times* reviewer Dilys Powell favourably compared the film to the 'Goon Shows' and Clive Barnes of the *Daily Express* to the Marx Brothers ('These boys are the closest thing to the Marx Brothers since the Marx Brothers'[35]), other critics were less forthcoming with their praise, attacking the film's frenetic narrative pace and lack of character development. For example, Nina Hibbin of the *Daily Worker* strongly criticized these elements, complaining that 'you find yourself sinking deeper and deeper into your seat, dazed, bemused, punch-drunk, defeated, limp.'[36] Likewise, Cecil Wilson of the *Daily Mail* was also unimpressed, maintaining that the film 'reduces them to robots' and complained that the vast array of visual jokes were 'like so many plums which fail somehow to merge into the pudding'.[37]

Despite a more lukewarm reception than was perhaps expected, the film still performed favourably at the British and American box-office, doing 'about as well'[38] as its predecessor and thrilling audiences with its inventive musical sequences. As Victor Spinetti remembers, 'You can never ever, once you've seen it, forget that 'Ticket to Ride' sequence. It burst onto the screen and it was magical. On the opening night, people just burst into cheering at the end of that sequence.'[39]

Likewise, the soundtrack material performed well, with the album retaining a number one position in Britain for nine weeks and the title track single for three. The other single release, 'Ticket to Ride', had been released some weeks before the film and also topped the British charts for three weeks. American sales were no less impressive and, despite the format differences mentioned earlier, the three film-related releases topped the *Billboard*, *Cashbox* and *Record World* charts. Moreover, the track 'Yesterday', which appeared on the British album and was released as a single in America, also topped the American charts, in Hertsgaard's words becoming the song which 'more than any other ... extended the Beatles' appeal beyond their initial core audience of young people and forced remaining mainstream sceptics to acknowledge that this band was no mere fad but a musical force to be reckoned with.'[40] Indeed, by 1995 it had long established itself as the most covered song of all-time, with well over two thousand versions in the thirty years since its release.[41] Ultimately for the Beatles, the success of the *Help!* film and soundtrack represented the pinnacle of their mass appeal as all-round family entertainers, and although the film was released just seven weeks after they had received their MBE awards, they would never appear this 'wholesome' again.

The release of the film also signalled the end of Lester's cinematic association with the Beatles as a group, although in the following year he went to Spain to make *How I Won the War* (1966), a deeply satirical anti-war comedy which included a minor role for John Lennon as the pacifist Private Gripweed. As Lester remembers, 'I didn't want to do another film with them because I felt that they had reached the stage that for both of us it would be right to go off on our own and not be continually linked.'[42] Moreover, as I shall discuss in the next chapter, the Beatles 'had reached the stage where they wanted much more control over their own destiny'.[43] Reflecting on his final Beatles movie, Lester maintains that he 'always preferred' *Help!* to *A Hard Day's Night* because he felt that it was a 'much harder job', and that 'it was not just an ordinary sequel'.[44] Indeed, although the film never attained the same critical status as its predeccesor, its brave and for the most part successful change of direction forces one to wonder what a third Beatles/Lester movie might have produced.

In the months following the film's commercial success, a number of ideas were discussed for the Beatles' next starring role in their third United Artists feature film project, although producer Walter Shenson was unable to find 'a script or storyline that everyone was able to agree on'.[45] At one point, it was announced that the next Beatles film was to be an adaptation of Richard Condon's Western, *A Talent for Loving*, but the idea was eventually dropped and subsequently produced elsewhere. Another idea which received serious discussion was a 'Three Musketeers' film, but again the project failed to progress beyond the planning stage since, in Shenson's words, the idea was 'rather corny and, thankfully, nobody wanted to do anything like that'.[46] Perhaps the most notorious unrealized script was developed by playwright Joe Orton in early 1967, shortly before the Beatles embarked on their own film-making venture. Orton had achieved considerable notoriety for provocative farces such as *Loot*, and had been contacted by Shenson with a view to developing an existing script for the new Beatles film. In January 1967 he was invited to dinner with Paul McCartney, who praised *Loot* despite maintaining that 'the only thing that I get from the theatre … is a sore arse'.[47] Orton's ideas grew and by February 1967 he had completed the first draft of a self-penned piece entitled *Up Against It*. The script, a predictably madcap and provocative cocktail of sex, politics and murder, was, however, considered unsuitable for the Beatles, and was returned to its author in early April without comment. 'Fuck them' was Orton's comment.[48]

Notes

1. See, for example, Hertsgaard, 1995, p. 106. Here the author describes the LP as the 'nadir of the group's recording efforts'.
2. Walker, 1986, p. 267.
3. Alun Owen interviewed in *Film Dope*, June 1993, p. 5.
4. Barrow, 1993a, p. 11.
5. Miles, 1978, p. 107.
6. Dick Lester, interviewed by author, 26 March 1996.
7. Joe McGrath, interviewed by author, 13 February 1996.
8. Dick Lester, interviewed by author.
9. Joe McGrath, interviewed by author.
10. Dick Lester, interviewed by author.
11. Ibid.
12. Ibid.
13. Ibid.
14. Ibid.
15. The Beatles' introduction to marijuana by Dylan is well documented in a number of sources. A detailed account can be found in Brown and Gaines, 1984, pp. 134–6.
16. Dick Lester, interviewed by author.
17. *Hollywood UK* (BBC, 1993).
18. Wenner, 1973, p. 20.
19. *Hollywood UK* (BBC, 1993).
20. *The Paul McCartney World Tour*, tour brochure, 1989, p. 47.
21. For example, see Brown and Gaines, 1984, pp. 147–8.
22. *The Paul McCartney World Tour*, 1989, p. 47.
23. *You Can't Do That: the Making of A Hard Day's Night* (VCI, 1994).
24. Dick Lester, interviewed by author.
25. Ibid.
26. Sheff, 1982, p. 150.
27. See, for example, Kozinn, 1995, p. 110.
28. Hertsgaard, 1995, p. 124
29. Sheff, 1982, p. 149.
30. MacDonald, 1994, p. 114.
31. Ann Pacey, 'Beatles You Put Me in a Flat Spin', *Sun*, 28 July 1965.
32. See, for example, Nina Hibbin, 'Come What May, You Cannot Crush a Beatle', *Daily Worker*, 7 July 1964. Here, Hibbin describes Ringo as the 'real comic of the quartet'.
33. Dick Lester, interviewed by author.
34. Starr, interviewed on *Aspel* (LWT, 1988).
35. Dilys Powell, 'Beatlage and Goonery', *Sunday Times*, 1 August 1965, and Clive Barnes, 'Marvellous – the Beatles' New Film', *Daily Express*, 28 July 1965. Powell maintains that the film is 'more successful in finding a visual equivalent to the verbal jungle of the Goons than such early TV attempts as *The Fred Shows*'.
36. Nina Hibbin, *Daily Worker*, 31 July 1965.
37. Cecil Wilson, *Daily Mail*, 28 July 1965.
38. Walker, 1986, p. 270.
39. Victor Spinetti, interviewed by author, 29 April 1996.
40. Hertsgaard, 1995, pp. 130–1.
41. Figure supplied by Beatles discographer, Neville Stannard.
42. Dick Lester, interviewed by author.
43. Ibid.
44. Ibid.
45. Somach, Somach and Muni, 1990, p. 133.
46. Ibid.
47. Lahr, 1980, p. 296.
48. Ibid., p. 311.

3

On the Road Again:
Magical Mystery Tour

The Beatles' next major movie project, the television film *Magical Mystery Tour*, began some two years after *Help!* and, unlike their previous productions, was self-produced, financed and directed. The concept of the film was initially proposed by Paul McCartney, who envisaged a semi-improvised fantasy musical in which the the group's most recent batch of soundtrack recordings would be sandwiched in a loose semi-comic and surreal narrative 'plot'. This 'plot', such as it was, consisted of a psychedelic day trip in which the Beatles, accompanied by a group of professional actors and performers, friends and fan club members travelled through unspecified parts of England in a multi-coloured bus, visiting such locations as an army recruitment centre, an Italian restaurant, and a Busby Berkeley-style musical set.

Although the idea was conceived by McCartney, the entire group was responsible for the 'story' of the film and, while much of the dialogue was improvised, the project was actually directed by all four Beatles, with Ringo Starr additionally credited as director of photography. Overseen by Apple Films' head Denis O'Dell, the film was produced for around £30,000[1] (over a two-week period) and released through Apple Films, a division of the group's emerging Apple business empire.

I have already discussed the economic and cultural reasons why film was (and still is) important to pop groups from a wider and more all-embracing economic perspective, but why should a group, with no previous experience of film-making (and with unlimited resources for hiring professional producers and directors), decide to write, direct and produce their own film? None of the Beatles has actually discussed reasons for such involvement in any depth, so one can only speculate as to how they became so deeply embroiled in the project. However, it is arguable that the group's interest in film-making at this point in their career was the result of both personal and wider, cultural factors.

From a personal perspective, they were rather unhappy with their previous film, *Help!*, and felt that their early 'loveable moptop' image had been over-exploited in both their previous vehicles. Referring to *Help!* and *A Hard Day's Night*, Lennon commented, 'We were a bit infuriated with the glibness and shiftiness of the dialogue [of *A Hard Day's Night*] and we were always trying to get it more realistic, but they wouldn't have it. It ended up OK, but the next one [*Help!*] was just bullshit because it really had nothing to do with the Beatles. They just put us here and there.'[2] He also said that the group 'felt like extras'[3] in their own film. By making their own film, the group may have felt that they would be retaining total artistic control over their product.

Lennon's dismissal of their early films suggests that he and the other members of the group felt that they did not have enough personal control over their image and artistic output. Moreover, their 1967 embrace of hippy counter-culture (using and, in McCartney's case publicly endorsing LSD,[4] supporting the underground press,[5] and taking classes in transcendental meditation[6]) seems to have been a reaction against five long years of being 'packaged' into a highly manufactured act which, while musically liberated, was heavily contrived (the identically besuited 'boy next door' image), politically censored (Epstein did not allow the group to discuss Vietnam publicly[7]), and domestically lionized (Harold Wilson's 1965 award to the group of the MBE). For the Beatles, the exploration of alternative lifestyles may have offered the attraction of an individualism and personal freedom paradoxically necessary to regain some semblance of sanity. The 'hippy' ideal distrusted the 'manufacturing' of mainstream pop culture and placed individualism, however ironically, high on its agenda, and the group's involvement with the movement could well have exaggerated their distrust of such promotional methods and accentuated their interest in self-production. Indeed, for all its potential hazards, self-production and direction provided the group with a golden opportunity to break out of the straitjacket of externally imposed media presentation, a presentation which, by 1965 and the release of *Help!*, had become basically repugnant to them.

Moreover, their supreme self-confidence in their ability to adapt to and master other media was, in 1967, at least theoretically justifiable within both their own biographical track record and, on a broader level, within the cultural and artistic climate of the period. Besides being the world's most successful contemporary songwriters and musicians, the Beatles justifiably saw themselves as cultural all-rounders, capable of mastering any medium which they felt inclined to dabble in. Quite apart from their music, each member had received considerable commercial and/or critical success for ventures undertaken outside the confines of the group itself. Lennon, for example, had published two best-selling books, while McCartney had provided the score for the Boultings' feature film *The Family Way* (1966). Meanwhile, Starr, keen to develop his acting career, had in August 1967 been offered a part in United Artists' new production, *Candy* (1968), a role which he accepted later in the year. He would later co-star with Peter Sellers in the dramatization of Terry Southern's novel, *The Magic Christian* (1969), in a role which, according to director Joe McGrath, was originally envisaged for Lennon.[8] Meanwhile Harrison had developed a profound interest in Indian music, and was busy mastering the sitar (an instrument which he brought into much of the Beatles' material from 1965) under the guidance of his musical guru, Ravi Shankar.

On a more conventionally musical level, the group were also achieving levels of commercial and critical success that, even in the early days of 'Beatlemania', they could not possibly have envisaged. Their most recent album release, *Sergeant Pepper's Lonely Hearts Club Band* (released in Britain on 1 June 1967), as well as being instantly heralded in all sectors of the media as a major artistic breakthrough in pop music's brief history, was also one of their biggest commercial successes to date.[9] With such multimedia success, it is hardly surprising that the group felt that a move into film-making would pose no serious problem. As McCartney somewhat naively stated before the completion of the show, 'Film-making isn't as difficult as many people imagine. It's a matter of common sense more than anything.'[10]

On a broader level, the Beatles' film-making venture could also have been influenced by the current climate of cross-fertilization and synergy which was taking place in pop art culture on a vast scale during the mid to late sixties, particularly in the avant-garde or 'intellectual' circles in which the Beatles, and particularly McCartney, mixed whilst living in St. John's Wood during this period. More than any previous period in British culture, the arts, and specifically the musical and visual arts, had become a fluid melting pot of inter-relationships, with each discipline influencing and affecting the others. While groups such as The Who absorbed the auto-destructive manifestos of Dadaism,[11] artists like Peter Blake borrowed from the imagery of youth culture, imbuing his work with iconography derived from fashion magazines and rock and roll memorabilia. Moreover, although the pop movement had no strict manifesto, its underlying ideology of instantaneous gratification, hedonism, industrial banality, youth culture and populism meant that artists such as Blake, Alan Aldridge and Richard Hamilton could comfortably cross over into other areas of design. Aldridge became art editor for Penguin Books in 1966, while Blake and Hamilton were involved in designing album covers for the Beatles in 1967 and 1968.[12] Other fine artists became even more experimental in the expansion of their media, and 'painters' such as Warhol (who visited McCartney circa 1966[13]) also worked in lithography, photography and film direction. While it is difficult to speculate upon the degree to which the contemporary cultural climate influenced the Beatles' move into film-making, it is clearly possible that the cross-fertilization in visual pop influenced their artistic sensibility.

Indeed, in many ways it is tempting to see their previous album release, *Sergeant Pepper*, as the epitome of such inter-disciplinary cross-fertilization, the 'product' itself comprising elements of music ('concept' songs by the Beatles), Blake's cover (which in its grandiose affluence, stylish montage and revolutionary 'gatefold' format self-consciously presented itself as 'art'), and literature (the printed lyrics of the songs, a first for a pop album, radically insisting that song lyrics should be considered as poetry). *Sergeant Pepper*'s release and enormous popularity crystallized the gradual shift in mainstream perceptions of pop music as a 'low' art, and ultimately elevated its cultural status to an intellectual level previously occupied by 'high' art such as theatre, literature and the fine arts. And if pop was now 'art', paradoxically art was now 'pop'. For the first time in pop music's brief history, it was embraced by intellectual and middle-class culture, and the avant-garde, a term paradoxically described by Lennon as being 'French for bullshit',[14] had become inextricably and harmoniously linked with popular teenage culture.

This cross-fertilization and popularization of the avant-garde or 'intellectual' arts (also mirrored by the heightened critical status of other media such as cinema and photography) was embraced by audiences and media alike, bridging cultural and generational differences and creating an overall pop culture which was both populist and avant-garde, elitist and classless, intellectual and anti-intellectual. Within a few short years, approaches and attitudes to culture had changed beyond all recognition. In his analysis of sixties culture, Christopher Booker discusses this aesthetic shift:

> [In 1956] there would have seemed an unbridgeable gulf between the concerns of, say, the teenagers jiving to Tommy Steele in the basement of the Two I's coffee bar and those of the audiences for Ionesco at the Royal Court Theatre. Now, in 1964, the coalescence of one form of fantasy with another to make up a sort of overall 'pop culture', was taking place so fast that, within a year or two, no-one would be surprised to see the pages of the 'quality' press regularly taken up with the rapturous reviews of the latest pop records, or prominent pop singers being starred in plays or films by directors of impeccable 'intellectual' credentials, such as Peter Hall or Jean Luc Godard – any more than they would be surprised to see Paul McCartney advertised as spending his leisure hours with the latest electronic fragment from the pen of Stockhausen.[15]

When in 1966 *Time* magazine boasted that London was fast becoming the most exciting city of the decade,[16] the exaggeration, for all its sensationalism and pretension, did not, at least on a cultural level, seem too jarring. The fusion of media, the synergy of styles and the spirit of youthful collaboration between artists from a vast array of disciplines and cultures meant that, at least for a brief period, the once risible idea of a 'swinging' London actually became a reality, and British pop culture, via the synergized commercial success of its musicians, designers, artists and photographers, became a highly exportable international phenomenon.

It is also possible that the group's decision to move into self-production and direction was based on a desire to counter the media's presumption that, with Epstein's death (on 27 August 1967), the Beatles, a product of his management, were also finished. Indeed, as Tony Barrow concedes, 'Epstein's death made the next thing the Beatles did absolutely crucial. The showbusiness world was watching to see how the group would handle itself without the personal management of their long-term mate and mentor, Brian Epstein.'[17] The Beatles' decision to become so heavily involved in a project which was (for them) experimental may have been influenced by a need to prove their doubters wrong in grand style, showing them that not only could they still produce successful music, they could also still turn their hand to any medium they chose. Although McCartney's initial ideas for the film's concept (which dated back to April 1967) had been discussed with and approved by Epstein before his death, it is not known whether the manager had approved of the idea of the Beatles as film directors. However, the fact that they decided to progress with the project so swiftly after his death gives rise to speculation that the group wished to allay popular doubts about their abilities as soon as possible.

The Beatles' mystery tour embarked on the first leg of the two-week shoot on 11 September 1967, heading for various locations in Hampshire, Devon, Cornwall and Somerset. Along with the cast members, the coach contained a skeleton crew of film technicians and of course the Beatles themselves, who remained on board throughout the first week of the 'tour'. After the first week of 'tour' shooting, filming continued at Paul Raymond's Revuebar in Soho and then switched to a disused hangar at West Malling Air Station which, in the absence of available studio space, served as a makeshift replacement for the sequences which required conventional sets. Here a number of notable sequences were shot, including the famous 'Walrus' sequence and the memorable sergeant-major scene featuring the Beatles' closest actor friend, Victor Spinetti, who was unable to take a bigger role in the film due to other acting commitments. As he remembers, 'I'd have loved to have gone on the whole trip, but I couldn't, and that was that. So John said, "Well, look, why don't you do that thing you do in *Oh! What a Lovely War*", the drill sergeant sketch which I did in that show, so I just reinvented it for the film.'[18]

Despite the alluring premise of keeping the project relatively small-scale, the smooth running of the shooting was hampered from the start by a number of technical and logistical problems. Convoys of news-hungry journalists pursued the coach relentlessly, and at one point it became stuck under a narrow bridge on a B road towards Dartmoor, resulting in huge tailbacks and flaring tempers. 'Fifth Beatle' Neil Aspinall encountered difficulties organizing the en-route accommodation, and there were also problems with the technicians union. Later, at West Malling, hearts dropped when, at around four o'clock on the last day of principal photography (24 September), the generators failed just as the cameras were to start rolling on the film's most complex and elaborate set piece, McCartney's 'Your Mother Should Know', causing delays while help was summoned by Denis O'Dell's assistant, Gavrik Losey. In the interim, Losey was mobbed when attempting to distribute signed photos to the 200 extras outside. Wherever they went, the Beatles were followed by hysterical fans. As Losey remembers, 'We were staying in a little hotel outside West Malling and the crowd that came pushed in the front window of the hotel... That level of adoration is just amazing to be around.'[19]

With principal shooting completed, the Beatles returned to London to begin working (under the supervision of Roy Benson) on the film's editing and to complete work on the soundtrack songs which they had begun before the start of shooting. Again there were problems. The editing took eleven weeks to complete (apparently because the group could never agree on the cutting[20]), and there were problems over how to present the songs which comprised the film's soundtrack. Although the previous Beatles film soundtracks had been issued on LPs with a second side of non-film songs, their stock of unreleased recordings had effectively run dry. Without the time to work on new material to make up a release of LP duration, they were left with the awkward problem of finding a solution for marketing the six recordings, which failed to fit into any recognized format.

After some discussion it was decided that the format of the record was to be a 'first' for the record industry, a double EP package encased in a twenty-four-page glossy booklet which contained the lyrics of the songs, stills from the film and a psychedelic cartoon strip (complete with captions) of the film's 'story'. The booklet was produced in association with the Beatles' official fan club, and carried an advertisement for both the club and its official monthly magazine, the *Beatles Monthly Book*, which had been running since 1963. While the accompanying booklet was in itself advertising for other Beatles-related merchandise for the unconverted who were not fan-club members, it also served another, more subtle 'reassuring' function for the 58,000 subscribers. With a booklet containing illustrations executed in a recognizably similar style to the black-and-white illustrations used to adorn the pages of the official fan club magazine, those who subscribed could feel reassured that their chosen publication was officially endorsed by the Beatles. The degree to which the format of the EP package was shaped solely by necessity is unknown. While it certainly solved the song quota problem, one suspects that it was also partly born of the Beatles' pioneering desire to experiment with conventional formats and packaging. Interestingly, although *Magical Mystery Tour* was never broadcast in America, the songs from the film did appear in LP format (also titled *Magical Mystery Tour*), augmented by five other recordings from the year which had already been issued as singles. This policy was not followed in Britain because it was considered exploitative to issue an album that was comprised of too many singles, and of the twenty-two singles released in Britain between 1962 and 1970 only about half contained music (from A or B side) pilfered from albums.

The EP was also artistically unprecedented for the group in that it was their first and only record to contain an instrumental number, 'Flying', which also became the only song to be co-written by all four members of the group. The other songs to be issued on the discs were 'Magical Mystery Tour', 'Blue Jay Way', 'I Am the Walrus', 'Your Mother Should Know' and 'The Fool on the Hill'. The record was eventually released on 8 December 1967 at a price of 19s 6d.[21]

With the benefit of almost thirty years' hindsight, the most striking formal aspect of *Magical Mystery Tour* is its radical lack of any remotely classical narrative structure. Indeed, if Lester's first film managed to provide a far looser and wayward narrative construction than previous pop musicals, *Magical Mystery Tour* takes this development one stage further, and marks a departure from constructed, classical narrative coherence, opting instead for a discourse which, for the most part, rejects conventional principles of logic and motivation. Indeed, the 'narrative' consists merely of a series of musical sequences intertwined with 'psychedelic' sequences which take place either on the coach or at various unspecified ports of call during the journey. There are no goal-oriented protagonists, there is no logically motivated cause-effect chain and, once the initial premise has been established (that we are going on a magical mystery tour), there is no attempt at any form of narrative resolution. Indeed, the 'resolution' merely consists of an 'unmotivated' cut from the interior of a strip club to a Busby Berkeley-style set where we see the group (dressed in white tuxedos and surrounded by dancers) performing a loosely choreographed dance to 'Your Mother Should Know'. Before 1967, such a sustained break with narrative logic and causality had not been attempted by the pop musical, and even now the formal style of *Magical Mystery Tour* seems quite radical. However, although much has been made of the group's lack of technical film-making expertise,[22] the film's radical form was clearly deliberate. The idea was that each member of the group should write unscripted sequences loosely related to the thematic premise of a fantasy coach trip (which could then be spontaneously improvised by whoever was acting in or directing the scene), and assembled, rather like a Dadaist collage, at the editing stage.[23] As McCartney maintained, 'We just got a lot of things ready and fitted them together.'[24] Indeed, as he explained some years later, 'I did a few little sketches myself and everyone else thought up a couple of little things. John thought of a little thing and George thought of a scene and we just kind of built it up.'[25]

Despite the lack of narrative coherence, the film enjoys an astonishing eclecticism and, like *A Hard Day's Night*, draws on a number of cinematic styles, happily jumping between, and at times combining, formal conventions from several different contemporary and historical genres. Despite their lack of practical film-making experience, the group were clearly not cinematically illiterate, as the sheer eclecticism of the film's style testifies. Perhaps the most obvious influence is that of surrealist cinema; and while surrealism had played an important part in the group's previous films, with *Magical Mystery Tour* it became far more pronounced and all-embracing. Besides the lack of narrative coherence, the film boasts many sequences which demonstrate a distinctly surreal influence. Indeed, in its affection for surreal imagery, one could easily argue that *Magical Mystery Tour* is visually closer in spirit to Dali and Buñuel's *Un chien andalou* (1928) than to any previous pop musical. Besides the surreal iconography of the mise-en-scene (the swaying policemen on the wall, the Beatles' unmotivated changes into animals, the sergeant shouting gibberish orders to a stuffed cow), there are sequences which seem heavily influenced by Dali and Buñuel's films, and just as their collaborations displace conventional ideas of cinematic space and perspective, so too does *Magical Mystery Tour*. Such is the case when Lennon and Harrison, accompanied by a number of their entourage, walk into a two-man tent only to find themselves in a cinema. Despite the difference of location, the scene bears a significant resemblance to a sequence in *Un chien andalou* in which the 'heroine', retreating from her lover, exits a suburban house to find herself on a beach. The film also makes constant use of the non-diegetic insert, and at various irregular intervals in the action we are greeted by a conventionally unmotivated shot of a cheering and waving crowd. While this formal trait can hardly be said to be 'surrealist' in its formal origins, it is employed with all the gratuitous anti-logic of a surrealist production, its effect further disengaging the viewer from any sense of conventional causality.

However, the film's affinity with surrealist dream imagery and narrative motivation is perhaps unsurprising when one considers two important factors. First, and perhaps most importantly, the Beatles had, as I noted earlier, become involved in mind-expanding drug culture. The aesthetics of psychedelia (to recreate visually or musically the effects of mind-expanding drugs) are closely related to those of surrealism, which recreates experiences unbound from the enslavement of reason. In 1967, no discernible genre of 'psychedelic' cinema existed, and it is natural that a group seeking to make a psychedelic film should turn to surrealist iconography for their inspiration. Moreover, while this is not to suggest that the film is not genuinely inspired or motivated by the 'psychedelic' aesthetic (as Lennon maintained in 1970, 'I must have had a thousand trips ... I used to just eat it [LSD] all the time'[26]), the relationship between psychedelia and surrealism became, at least for the Beatles, inseparable. As Lennon once commented, 'Surrealism had a great effect on me ... psychedelic vision is reality to me.'[27] Indeed, Lennon was particularly impressed by the surrealist films of Buñuel, and Victor Spinetti accompanied him to screenings of *Belle de Jour* (1967).[28] Indeed, it is clearly possible that the group's writing technique of randomly joining sections of unrelated narrative events is partly derived from André Breton and Paul Eluard's writing game, 'The Exquisite Corpse', which randomly linked non-related or loosely related group writing to produce surrealist narrative. A similar random technique was partly employed to enlist the professional actors used in the production. The group selected cast members by flicking through the pages of the actors' directory 'Spotlight', and employed them on the strength of looks rather than any reasoned investigation of ability or track record. On a non-textual level, it is also interesting to note that the insignia for Apple, the Beatles' production company, was also inspired by surrealist art, namely a Magritte painting brought to McCartney's house by gallery owner Robert Fraser around 1966.

The writing and recording techniques employed for the more psychedelic songs on the film's soundtrack also owe a debt to surrealist and Dadaist form, and this is particularly apparent in the film's most lavish production, Lennon's 'I Am the Walrus'. Indeed, while the form of Lennon's lyric is clearly indebted to the unconscious nonsense poetry and 'automatic' writing style of the surrealists, the recording techniques are clearly derived from the Dadaist chance aesthetic. Just as artists such as Jean Arp produced paintings such as *Squares Arranged by Chance* (1917) by throwing pieces of paper in the air and glueing them to their landing spot, so George Martin's pioneering production work applied similar techniques: whilst recording the earlier *Sergeant Pepper* LP, the producer had created an atmospheric soundwash for the backing track of 'Being For the Benefit of Mr Kite' by cutting up tapes from the sound stock library of EMI and sticking them randomly back together. Although not constructed in exactly the same manner, the recording of parts of 'I Am the Walrus' was created with a similar 'chance' aesthetic, and amongst its many backing effects the song features radio interference and excerpts from a BBC radio production of *King Lear*, found on the radio tuning dial by Lennon during the song's re-mix and randomly fed into the backing track.

Finally, it is possible that the surrealist/psychedelic aesthetic also had a considerable impact upon the presentation of the group's songs in the musical sequences. Prior to the film's conception, the majority of British and American pop musicals had, as we have noted, relied upon the long-established tradition of presenting musical numbers as authentic performances. While the first pop musical to break the conventions of the performance-based tradition was arguably the Beatles' own *A Hard Day's Night*, *Magical Mystery Tour* can lay claim to being one of the first pop musicals to feature a soundtrack which almost completely negated the idea of 'realistic' performance.

Indeed, apart from the humorous 'Walrus' sequence, which I will discuss later, few of the other musical sequences make the remotest attempt to simulate a conventionally 'realistic' diegetic group or vocal performance, with the remaining songs often acting as a non-diegetic soundtrack to accompany the surreal action. 'Flying', for example, does not feature any of the Beatles at all, and the sequence for 'Fool on the Hill' is accompanied by footage of McCartney walking around the French countryside, intercut with occasional close-ups of his eyes peering deeply into the camera. Even when there is some conformity to the performance aesthetic (as in the 'I Am the Walrus' and 'Blue Jay Way' sequences), there is only the slightest attempt to realistically lip-sync the songs, as if the vocalists are actually parodying the artificiality of classical miming.

While this is clearly in line with the surrealist aesthetic, it may also be related to the group's volatile relationship with the BBC, the channel on which the film was screened. Apart from banning 'A Day in the Life' earlier in 1967, the organization had vetoed the McCartney-directed promo film for their single 'Hello, Goodbye' from its weekly chart show, *Top of the Pops*, on the grounds that it showed the group lip-synching to a backing track, and therefore contravened the Musicians' Union miming rule (implemented in 1966) and which ruled that non-conceptual television appearances should be 'live'. Although the clip clearly showed the Beatles lip-synching, the group subsequently made every effort to comply with the BBC and, on 21 November 1967, allowed them to shoot some footage of the group editing *Magical Mystery Tour* on the understanding that this, along with some stills provided by NEMS, could then be edited into the clip to cover the most obviously lip-synched segments. However, claiming that there had been too little time to edit the 'new' clip together, the BBC annoyed the Beatles by using footage from *A Hard Day's Night* to accompany the clip on its first transmission (23 November), and subsequently employing a combination of the stills/editing footage without any of the performance material.[29] As a television film, *Magical Mystery Tour* was not subject to the same regulations, and it is possible that the exaggerated lack of sound/vision synchronization was a satirical parody of such bureaucratic pettiness.

However, we should not ignore the possible influence of more contemporary forms of surrealism on *Magical Mystery Tour*. Although, as I have suggested, it is most likely that the group's interest in surrealism was born largely from a direct interest in integrating elements of its 'pure', 'first generation' form, the Beatles, like any other artists, did not work in a cultural or historical void. While it would perhaps be an overstatement to suggest that the sixties heralded a surrealist revival, the aesthetic of anti-logic had become increasingly pervasive in radio and television comedy since the fifties, and the emergence of the *Goon Shows*. As I noted earlier, the Beatles were great fans of the surreal and anarchic humour of the Goons, and particularly

Lester's own collaboration with them on the silent movie parody, *The Running, Jumping and Standing Still Film*. Like *Magical Mystery Tour*, *The Running, Jumping and Standing Still Film* has its roots in surrealism, and frequently integrates its aesthetic into visual humour. As Alexander Walker maintains, it is littered with 'surrealist gags like the scrubbing brush used on the grass, the inverted logic of racing round a stationary phonograph disc with a needle, the ramshackle nationalism of the box-kite decorated with Union Jacks as Britain's entry to the space race, and the famous subversive booby-trap that beckons a distant figure nearer and nearer till he is within reach of the boxing glove on the hand outside the frame.'[30] *Magical Mystery Tour* shares a similar interest in visual surrealist humour, and it is certainly possible that such throwaway jokes as the photographer's mutation into a lion were influenced by the Goons' idiosyncratic employment of its form.

Despite the clear influence of surrealism and Dada, the film also includes a number of scenes which are formally derived from more conventional genres, and there are sequences which demonstrate a tendency toward the direct cinema/realist tradition. Perhaps the best example of this can be found in the sequence which directly follows the 'I Am the Walrus' number, in which Lennon and Harrison, shot by hand-held camera, are seen blowing up a balloon for a little girl to play with. This tendency towards capturing seemingly unscripted and improvised action, together with the group's deliberate employment of a partly non-professional cast, could have been influenced by a number of loosely realist approaches which came to prominence in a variety of contemporary British and American productions. Indeed, while their own film debut had employed certain pseudo-realist techniques, contemporary directors such as Ken Loach were also incorporating realist methods (use of non-actors and improvised script) into film and television dramas such as *Cathy Come Home* (1966) and *Poor Cow* (1967). Another possible influence could come from D. A. Pennebaker's presentation of Bob Dylan's 1965 British tour, *Don't Look Back* (1966). Apart from the Rolling Stones and Elvis Presley, Bob Dylan was, throughout most of the sixties, the Beatles' only serious commercial rival, and as personal friends they would have watched his presentation with great interest. So it is clearly possible that the grainy, instantaneous qualities of Pennebaker's direct cinema also influenced the more objective 'fly-on-the-wall' sequences of *Magical Mystery Tour*.

Finally, and perhaps most importantly, the Beatles, like many, took advantage of contemporary technological innovation, and were avid home-movie makers. They took home-movie making very seriously, considering it to be an 'art' comparable with any other, McCartney even arranging a screening of his films for Antonioni whilst he was in London to shoot *Blow-up* (1966). As Joe McGrath remembers, Lennon was also a great home-movie enthusiast, carrying a small 8mm camera with him wherever he went with the progressive and (as it has since transpired) somewhat prophetic philosophy that 'there will come a time when you will be able to use a film camera like a biro. You take it out, you use it and then you put it away again.'[31] It is perfectly possible that the group wanted to include home-movie-style footage in the film to elevate (what they considered to be) its artistic credibility by placing it into a professional context. On a more practical level, it was also a manner of shooting with which they had some direct experience, and therefore presumably the mode of film-making with which they felt most comfortable.

The film also pastiches a number of other genres, most notably the family fantasy film and the thirties Hollywood musical. Indeed, if the sequences of the Beatles as four magicians who cast 'wonderful magical spells' on the bus is reminiscent of fairytale folklore, then the final sequence is clearly a pastiche of the thirties *Gold Diggers* series, choreographed and shot in the same style as the Busby Berkeley musicals. It is interesting here to compare writing and performing with the Beatles' fondness for musical pastiche, as it seems that their fascination with writing and performing songs in the style of other artists is echoed by the cinematic pastiche of *Magical Mystery Tour*. This is particularly true of McCartney's songwriting style, and it is clearly no coincidence that the writer of such music-hall pastiche as 'When I'm Sixty Four' should have conceived and scored the 'Hollywood' sequence at the film's closure. Indeed, just as it is possible to see *Sergeant Pepper* as a record born of a pastiche sensibility, one might say the same for parts of *Magical Mystery Tour*. The originality of both record and film lay in their constant fascination with and haphazard absorption of the formal language of other genres. Just as *Sergeant Pepper* was the first rock and roll record to be paradoxically preoccupied and inspired by any other musical genre than rock and roll, so *Magical Mystery Tour* is the first pop musical to be so utterly absorbed by formal styles other than those of the genre (or generic precedents) to which it should, at least in theory, belong. Indeed, although their first film was partly instrumental in initiating the possibilities for the pop musical to achieve this, *Magical Mystery Tour* marks the Beatles' own realization and employment of this aesthetic, and its pastiche sensibilities were probably as influenced by their recording approach as by their previous film-making experience. As McCartney commented in 1973, 'It was just like making a record album, that's how we did it anyway... A record is sound and a film is visual, that's the only difference.'[32]

Perhaps this comment provides the biggest clue as to why the group should make a film which is so fond of pastiche and so anti-institutional in its narrative form. The Beatles approached film-making in predominantly the same way as they approached sound recording, and although their interest in counter-culture was, along with their previous film-making experiences, clearly partly responsible for the anti-institutional nature of the narrative, my suspicion, which would seem to be enforced by McCartney's comments, is that the highly experimental nature of the film's form is also a logical extension of the anti-classical, progressive nature of their songwriting and recording techniques. As well as presenting popular music as 'art', *Sergeant Pepper* is frequently canonized as the record which, on its most simplistic level, transformed rock and roll (music to dance to) into rock ('serious' music to listen to). *Magical Mystery Tour* attempted something similar in its own genre and, despite its intended comedy element, the film's form marks a radical departure from the conventionality and frivolous boyishness of pop musicals prior to its conception. It demanded that pop musicals need not conform to formulaic precedents and, in so doing, attempted to do the same for the pop musical as *Sergeant Pepper* had already done for pop music. It suggested that the genre could also be approached as a self-conscious and serious 'art' which demanded an active, rather than passive, audience.

Ian MacDonald, in his discussion of *Magical Mystery Tour*, describes the 'subversive agenda' of the film, claiming that the Beatles were 'sending up consumerism, showbiz, and the clichés of the media' in 'their version of the counter-culture's view of mainstream society'.[33]

No strand of sixties culture was homogeneous, and the much discussed counter-culture or 'underground' youth culture was comprised of a number of different strands which embraced political, religious, spiritual and moralist/humanist, and drug-oriented sub-cultures.[34] However, despite their different premises, each strand shared a common distrust of the establishment. The 'version' of counter-culture which inspired the Beatles in 1967 was essentially a loose amalgamation of consciousness-expanding ideas culled from an array of alternative sub-cultures. Indeed, as Hanif Kureishi has noted, the group acted as 'popularizers' of a range of 'esoteric ideas' concerning politics, mysticism and drug use.[35]

Despite its deliberate lack of narrative causality, the film seems charged with a deeply satirical mockery of both the establishment and 'straight' society. While this is obviously reflective of the general nature of counter-culture, the Beatles' ideological motivation was probably further accentuated by contemporary attempts to calm the 'movement' they had embraced. Discussing 1967's 'summer of love', Ian MacDonald maintains:

> It was then that the British establishment, disconcerted by the explosion of counter-culture in the UK and aware of the unrest and civil disobedience associated with its parent movement in America, moved to stifle it at home by making examples of its leading representatives (notably the underground paper *International Times*, raided for 'subversive material' by the police in March). Though the MBE-inoculated Beatles were immune, their outrageous colleagues the Rolling Stones were fair game and within months Mick Jagger and Keith Richards were arrested on drugs charges... Soon after this, despite an outcry from the country's younger generation, Britain's hugely popular and perfectly harmless 'pirate' radio stations were officiously banned. The times they were a-changing.[36]

How, then, is the satirical mockery of conventional society and the establishment achieved? More often than not, it is accomplished through surrealist pastiche, and just as the films of Dali and Buñuel used surreal imagery and scenarios to mock the morality of Catholicism, so *Magical Mystery Tour* employs similar devices, creating surreal sequences which mock (albeit more gently) the morality of all pillars of conventional British society, including state authorities such as the law and the military, organized Christianity, sexual censorship, and 'straight' working-class notions of entertainment and leisure. Indeed, if the film's narrative construction can be said to be violently anti-institutional, then so too can its ideology.

Perhaps the most poignant example of the mockery of state authorities is the sequence in which the party stop off in an army recruitment office, only to be confronted by a Sergeant (Victor Spinetti) who aggressively shouts abstract, meaningless orders at the entourage until Ringo gently asks 'why?' The scene then cuts to a similar sequence in which the same character is seen attempting to impose his gibberish orders upon a stuffed cow which is mounted on the back of a plank. The police are similarly ridiculed and, just as the surrealist films mocked religious figures by placing them into incongruous and childish imagic contexts, so *Magical Mystery Tour* does the same: the dancing policemen in the 'Walrus' sequence are employed in the same manner as the piano-chained priests of *Un chien andalou*. The Church of England is lampooned in a similar manner in the marathon sequence, in which a group of argumentative vicars are seen to be making unpleasant gestures at the winners of the race. However, while it is tempting to regard *Magical Mystery Tour* as uniquely subversive in such surreal satire, it is important to remember that the mockery of establishment figures and state authorities had already been partly culturally legitimised by the media, and especially television. Indeed, just as the sixties heralded something of a rebirth for a formally surrealist comic aesthetic via the Goons, so it also ushered in the start of the satire boom. Although informed by a totally different formal and ideological aesthetic (most shows had no pre-planned ideological agenda and indiscriminately satirized anything), the inclusion of skits and sketches which mocked leading political figures and other institutional icons had already pervaded factions of the nation's consciousness via such programmes as BBC TV's *That Was the Week That Was* (1962–3) and Rediffusion's *At Last the 1948 Show* (1967). The latter, essentially a comedy show comprised of satirical skits devised by ex-Cambridge performers such as John Cleese, Graham Chapman and Tim Brooke-Taylor, shared the Beatles' love of surrealist satire, and although much of its comedy was verbal, its sketches demonstrated a similar formal interest in the iconography of the absurd.

However, apart from mocking the symbolic representatives of state power, *Magical Mystery Tour* also satirizes slightly less predictable institutional concepts, such as traditional working-class notions of showbusiness and leisure, and it is likely that the group were again informed by a loose hippy ideal which distrusted conventional capitalist notions of ordinary 'entertainment' and placed emphasis upon 'free' spontaneous 'happenings' such as 'love-ins' and 'be-ins'.[37] The reason the group should choose to satirize working, rather than middle-class notions of these concepts, is probably twofold. First, if, as I suspect, the ideological intention of the narrative was to apolitically satirize all factions of 'straight' or 'square' society, then in the interest of balance (or just plain satirical anarchy) there was no reason why mainstream working-class culture should be excluded. Secondly, and from a purely biographical perspective, such forms of entertainment were particularly familiar to the upper-working-class roots of the Beatles, who, before their rise to fame in 1962, had spent their formative years playing on the British and German club and cabaret circuit.

Accordingly, the film is littered with instances which seem gently, and often affectionately, to satirize the professional insincerity and contrived prowess of traditionally working-class entertainments, including nightclub and cabaret acts as well as the actual notion of the mystery tour, itself a popular form of working-class entertainment. Indeed, this is apparent from the very beginning, and Lennon's introductory voice-over ('When a man buys a ticket for a magical mystery tour he knows exactly what he's going to get, the trip of a lifetime'), which is delivered in a sarcastic tone. Moreover, the speeches of the courier, Jolly Jimmy Johnson ('All my friends call me Jolly Jimmy, and you are all my friends'), can be read as a gentle satire on the insincerity of the leisure industry, while the drunken, unsynched performance of Bonzo's vocalist Vivian Stanshall as the crass crooner in the nightclub appears to ridicule the tired routines of traditional cabaret entertainment, portraying it as grotesquely amateurish and completely insincere.

The film also attempts to lambast traditional conventions of British censorship and moral 'taste'. As has already been noted, the group's direct and indirect output came under considerable scrutiny from such organizations as the BBC, who had recently banned 'I Am the Walrus' from their playlists on the grounds that certain lines were judged to be sexually obscene. As such it is possible that the animated 'censored' sign which covers stripper Jan Carson's breasts in the nightclub sequence is a slyly satirical dig at both the BBC and self-righteous moral crusaders such as Mary Whitehouse, whose 1964 Clean Up TV Campaign had produced, in Arthur Marwick's terms, a 'running battle between the advocates of permissiveness and tolerance and those of purity and censorship.'[38] The sequence had allowed the Beatles, as advocates of the former, to have their cake and eat it. It showed 'offensive' permissiveness, and was therefore loosely in keeping with their advocacy of 'free' love, yet because of its humorous animation it could not be banned for sexual obscenity.

In tandem with the satirical treatment of 'straight' society is the promotion of 'alternative' lifestyles; and, bearing in mind the Beatles' frequent experimentation with mind-expanding substances, it is tempting to interpret the film's fundamental literal concept of the 'magical trip' as a thinly disguised metaphor for drug culture, the 'magic' being a metaphor for LSD and the 'trip' (already a loaded ideological term) being its effects. Moreover, it is clearly salient that it is only when experiencing the effects of the 'magical spells' from 'away in the clouds' that the entourage can truly enjoy themselves and achieve heightened levels of satisfaction. Indeed, the film occasionally switches between discernibly psychedelic fantasy/reality (or 'drugged/clean') modes, with objective reality exposed as dull and mundane. A fine example of this is the sequence on the bus which builds up to the 'Flying' extravaganza which, with its colour-filtered cloud images, closely resembles a simulated 'trip'. Here, the tour guide Miss Winters announces that 'if you look to your left the view is not very inspiring' (cut to shot of real, and genuinely uninspiring, landscape). 'Ah, but if you look to your right...' (cut to colour-filtered clouds which herald the start of the 'Flying' sequence). Interestingly, the footage for this sequence included unused material shot some years earlier by Stanley Kubrick for *Dr Strangelove* (1964). The material, which was culled from hours of unused cloud formation footage, was now library footage and was subsequently purchased by production chief Denis O'Dell and tinted to achieve its psychedelic effect.[39] Shortly after the film was released, O'Dell received a call from Stanley Kubrick asking what right he had to use the footage. 'I was amazed,' remembers O'Dell with justified amusement. 'I thought, this man is a bloody genius, he'd remembered everything he'd shot!'[40]

By switching between modes, the film suggests that only when experiencing altered states of reality can life be bearable, and it is clearly significant that all the numerous arguments between Ringo and his

Aunty Jessie take place only when the film is in 'real' *cinéma-vérité* mode. In this way, it is possible to see *Magical Mystery Tour* as a fantasy fundamentally based on pure Leary-inspired wish-fulfilment, the idea being that 'ordinary' individuals can only receive a state of heightened awareness and spritual salvation through the 'magic' of mind-expanding drugs.

Interestingly, several writers have noted a connection between the fictitious concept of *Magical Mystery Tour* and a factual hippy 'happening' of the mid-sixties, namely the antics inspired by notorious novelist and acid-head, Ken Kesey, who was later to spend some time writing at Apple. As Mike Evans explains, 'The concept of the mystery tour, touring the country in a multi-coloured bus, had much in common with a seminal "happening" in the annals of the American drug culture – the 1966 LSD-fed trip [across America] of Ken Kesey's Merry Pranksters [a group of stoned hippies] in a day-glo bus, documented in Tom Wolfe's *Electric Kool-Aid Acid Test* (1968).'[41] Whether the Beatles were inspired by this incident is a question which will probably always remain unanswered. However, the concept for the film was conceived by McCartney when on a flight returning from America, shortly after Wolfe's reports had been first published in the *World's Tribune Journal* (in January and February 1967). As a fellow advocate of underground culture, it is likely that he would have taken an interest in such stories, and the similarities between the two concepts do seem more than coincidental.

Coinciding with the film's anti-institutional message is the group's chosen representation of themselves and, just as elements of the narrative mirror the group's newly acquired taste for elements of the counter-culture, so too does the nature of the Beatles' filmic image, as expounded by their costume, behaviour, performance and songs. As I noted earlier, between the release of *Help!* and *Magical Mystery Tour* they had, like many other contemporary groups, become influenced by the doctrines of meditation and LSD, and this totally changed their musical style, media presentation and public image. Although it is possible to trace the group's interest in these subjects back to their 1966 album release, *Revolver*,[42] it was not until 1967, and the release of *Sergeant Pepper*, that the Beatles became universally regarded as the leaders of psychedelic music and fashion. Moreover, this was accentuated by the broadcast and success of their mid-1967 single 'All

You Need is Love', the anthemic Western mantra which, in its idealistic appeal for global harmony, became the ultimate universal slogan of the 'flower power' era. It appealed to all factions of mainstream culture and also managed to transcend the divisions of the contemporary underground movements which, already deeply impressed by the group's popularization of ethnic fashions and radical endorsement of 'alternative' lifestyles, regarded the Beatles as their 'supreme spokesmen'.[43] However, despite such popularity, by December 1967 and the release of *Magical Mystery Tour* the Beatles had gone a long way towards destroying their previous mid-sixties image as clean-cut and 'wholesome' family entertainers. They no longer appeared on 'kiddiepop' television shows answering questions about their favourite colours, and they no longer pandered to the banal questioning of the tabloid press. And when the Beatles did give their attention to the media, it often had more to do with the promotion of alternative lifestyles such as meditation or drug culture than their latest record or film releases. In October and September they discussed Transcendental Meditation on the *David Frost Show*, and they helped finance, and signed, a 'legalize pot' advertisement in a July 1967 edition of *The Times*. They gave exclusive and increasingly philosophical interviews to the underground press, and in late 1967 they announced the opening of the Apple boutique, a hippy shop designed to be a 'beautiful place where you can buy beautiful things'.[44]

In two short years, the Beatles' visual, musical and philosophical image had changed beyond recognition. They had shed their Pierre Cardin suits of the early 'Beatlemania' days, and their dress became a visual explosion of psychedelic Technicolor which encompassed Afghan coats, Pickwick jackets, granny specs and floral shirts. Their increasingly complex and innovative music was still popular with a cross-generational audience, but their attempts to popularize less mainstream ideas reflected the fact that they had now outgrown and rejected any desire to be seen as the establishment's role model for youth; by late 1967, it was unthinkable that only two years earlier they had been awarded the MBE, and even the Queen commented that 'the Beatles are turning awfully funny, aren't they?'[45]

Now an international phenomenon of unparalleled importance and, since Epstein's death, without a manager to impart suggestions or impose decisions upon them, the Beatles were free to break from their previously imposed cinematic image of cheeky conformity and to present themselves however they wished. Gone was the boyish 'family favourite' image of *Help!* and *A Hard Day's Night*, only to be replaced by a self-presentation which, informed by their new philosophical outlook, was consciously or subconsciously committed to demolishing public perceptions of the 'cute' boy-next-door image once and for all. How, then, was the group's presentation in the film informed by counter-culture, and how exactly did this presentation differ from their previous incarnations in the cinema?

Perhaps the most striking aspect of the Beatles' image in *Magical Mystery Tour* is that it broke with their previous tradition of appearing in films as 'themselves', and attempted to scramble any sense of identificatory perception by mixing footage of dramatic action in which they appear as actors who play characters within a dramatic context, sequences where they appear as 'themselves' in a dramatic or performance-based context, and sequences where the distinction is unclear. For example, Ringo Starr appears as an actor who plays one of the five magicians, as 'himself' (as drummer of the Beatles in the 'Walrus' sequence), and as 'Richard B. Starkey', a part which associates Ringo's real name and alter ego with that of a fictional character, the hen-pecked nephew of Aunty Jessie. In this way, the viewer's perception of the group is constantly blurred by a series of dramatic and non-dramatic paradoxes which partially obscure any single and coherent image of the Beatles as a 'pop group'. This 'multiple-image' strategy performs a dual role. While it is clearly in keeping with the underground principle of satirizing conventional showbusiness 'manufacturing' and modes of representation, it also allows them the personal freedom to escape from the singly contrived group persona presented in *Help!* and *A Hard Day's Night*. Again, it is interesting to make comparisons with the group's musical career, and just as *Magical Mystery Tour* partially allowed the group to work as actors in a dramatic context, so the playful masquerade of *Sergeant Pepper* allowed them to 'act' within a musical context (i.e. to perform songs under a guise which partially subverted their recognizable identity as 'the Beatles').

Moreover, when the group do appear as 'themselves' (either within the dramatic context or when 'performing' songs), their image marks a total departure from the imposed boyishness and cheeky conformity of their previous cinematic excursions. Indeed, just as the film can, at least partially, be read as a surreal/psychedelic indictment of 'straight' society, so the Beatles' self-image can be seen as an advertisement *for* mysticism, drug culture, individualism and general non-conformity. While these concepts were all gleaned from separate strands of Anglo-American counter-culture, the Beatles managed to combine them harmoniously into a highly potent ideological cocktail which seemed to amalgamate elements of hippy drug culture, Eastern philosophy and underground satire into a single self-image. Perhaps the best example of this amalgamation of styles and ideologies can be seen in Harrison's sequence for 'Blue Jay Way', which contains elements from an array of alternative sub-cultures, however fundamentally ideologically opposed. While he appears to be visibly 'tripping' (and therefore presenting himself as a Leary-inspired advocate of mind-expanding drugs), his 'lotus' posture also implies a contradictory advocacy of spiritual purity via transcendental mysticism and meditation. Moreover, he also appears to be 'playing' a keyboard drawn on the pavement where he sits, again a possible piece of underground satire on the banality of artifice which would probably have appealed to readers of *IT* and *Oz*. The fact that he appears unaccompanied by any other group member stresses the wider, and more populist, hippy cliché of 'doing your own thing', and the playful phonetic metamorphosis of the song's final lengthy refrain seemingly imparts a similar message of individualism and rejection of social conformity. Apart from the dramatic action itself, the iconography of the group's costumes also manages to compromise the fashions of different youth sub-cultures. This is particularly apparent in the 'Walrus' sequence, where the costumes (almost certainly designed by the Dutch collective 'The Fool'[46]) combine the bright, 'high fashion' day-glo colours of psychedelic styles with the ethnic Eastern iconography of genuine Indian wear.

The degree to which the group could justifiably be called 'opportunistic' in their reconciliation of seemingly opposing strands of fashionable youth sub-culture is a question as unresolvable as it is unimportant. What is certain is that their presentation in *Magical Mystery Tour* confirmed and crystallized the Beatles' recently acquired media image as the central figureheads of their own all-embracing, and therefore paradoxically populist, vision of counter-culture.

One final and important question remains unanswered. Given that the Beatles had an audience which transcended age and culture, why would they make an 'underground' film which, in its form and ideology, seemed to deliberately marginalize their following? Granted, they had become, in Melly's terms, genuine 'underground converts',[47] and yes, they had been dissatisfied with the imposed and contrived image of their previous screen incarnations. But surely, as a highly astute and intelligent group of musicians who were now beginning to branch into the business world, were they not committing financial and commercial suicide?

Prior to shooting the film, the Beatles announced that *Magical Mystery Tour* would be a film for an 'all-inclusive, non-exclusive'[48] audience, presumably meaning that it would attempt to cater for all ages and factions of its potentially massive audience. That the Beatles clearly felt that they did not need to attempt to make a traditional musical which was remotely conventionally commercial or obviously 'all-inclusive' is a testament to their godhead status as popularizers, rather than followers, of commercial trends. After all, prior to its release, everything the Beatles had produced had achieved massive success, regardless of whether projects were conventionally 'commercial' or not. Indeed, at this point in their career it must have seemed to the group that the more experimental and anti-institutional the form and ideology of their work, the greater its potential critical and commercial popularity. For example, 'Yesterday', with its baroque string arrangement, was in its day a totally unconventional musical form for a pop group, yet it had popularized the classical ballad in mainstream pop and was fast becoming the most covered song of all time. By the same token, *Sergeant Pepper* was, in its day, extraordinarily radical musically, yet it had been extremely popular with both press and public. Moreover, as we have seen, the group's previous screen excursions had also, albeit more modestly, broken formal and ideological ground. The reality of the matter is that throughout their entire career up to this point the key ingredient for the Beatles' success had been their willingness to experiment with new forms and ideologies and to constantly change their image and style. Although their advocacy of certain ideas had brought them into considerable disrepute with sections of the public and the media, it had never harmed the critical or commercial reception of their work. As Britain's cultural royalty, they had no serious reason to believe that *Magical Mystery Tour* would be treated any differently. If anything, wouldn't its 'anti-commercialism' paradoxically make it more popular?

The critical reception of *Magical Mystery Tour* was (and still is) unprecedented in the Beatles' career. The film was almost unanimously savaged by critics and audiences alike and, for the first and only time in their career, the Beatles had to defend their work before a bewildered and angry British media. Indeed, as Philip Norman maintains, 'For the first time in their existence, the Beatles were unpopular.'[49] If anything, 'unpopular' is an understatement. Almost all the 'serious' and tabloid press ran cover stories such as 'Beatles' Mystery Tour Baffles Viewers',[50] and according to the *Daily Mirror* both the newspapers' and the BBC's switchboards were jammed by complaints from fans and impartial viewers alike.[51] Even *Melody Maker* (a magazine whose youthful readership extended beyond the usual conservatism of the press) received letters of complaint from bemused viewers, one of whom described it as the 'biggest disappointment of 1967'.[52]

The scale of the film's critical failure in Britain had serious commercial consequences for its overseas release, not least with the wealthy American television networks, who, besides being potentially high-paying buyers, also held the key to the film's largest affluent audience. On 28 December 1967, the *Los Angeles Times* ran a headline which read 'Beatles Produce First Flop with Yule Film', and although the television rights were sold to Japan, Australia and some European countries, the American networks, discouraged by the film's unfavourable British reception, backed out of lucrative sales negotiations at the eleventh hour, which meant that the film was not even seen by its most important target audience.[53] However, one wonders if this was actually a blessing in disguise. After all, although the group reputedly lost around $1 million in exhibition fees,[54] the American soundtrack became one of the fastest sellers in Capitol's history, grossing an enormous $8 million within just ten days,[55] in a country where the accompanying film went unseen. By comparison, the 'advertised' double EP set was less successful (by Beatles standards[56]) in Britain, becoming one of their few recordings which failed to top the *Record Retailer* charts. Considering the film as part of a package intended to generate 'direct' and related revenue, one would therefore have to concede that by the standards of their previous excursions into film, its critical and commercial failure was nothing short of monumental. Indeed, while 'relative' is clearly the operative word when discussing the film's economic failure (obviously American soundtrack royalties alone would easily have covered the modest production budget), one might argue that its singularly paradoxical commercial 'success' was that it was *not* shown in a country which I suspect would have reacted in much the same manner as the British audiences and critics.

Why, then, did critics and audiences despise the film so much? On a superficial level, the most obvious answer is that the form was simply too radical for its audiences' expectations, and it is certainly true that a considerable number of the criticisms and complaints arose from its unconventional narrative and anti-institutional plot. As a *Daily Mirror* story explained, 'By the thousand, viewers protested to the BBC who screened the fifty-minute film. What was it all about? they asked.'[57] TV pundits such as James Thomas of the *Daily Express* were also perplexed and angered by its form, complaining that 'the confusion was horrific'.[58] It is clearly evident, then, that both public and critics fatally attempted to judge the film in relation to the more conventional narrative entertainment they would normally expect from the group, and were either unable or unwilling to sympathize with the experimental nature of the film on its own terms. Indeed, the press, armed with the knowledge that the film had been assembled hastily and largely without a professional production crew, seemed to misconstrue experimentalism as amateurism, with critics from papers such as the *Daily Mirror* and the *Daily Express* implying that the avant-garde nature of the film's form was born out of the group's lack of film-making expertise and contempt for the public rather than any deliberate attempt to create something 'different'.[59] Jumping to the film's defence, McCartney attempted to explain its experimental nature in an intense series of press interviews and television appearances. Speaking to the *Daily Express* on 28 December, he maintained that 'the mistake was that too many people tried to understand it. There was no plot, so it was pointless trying to find one. It is like an abstract painting.'[60] To the *Daily Mirror* he added, 'Everybody was looking for a plot but purposely it wasn't there. The more people kept seeking a plot the worse it must have become for them. We did it as a series of disconnected, unconnected events.'[61]

Unsurprisingly, because they failed to comprehend the nature of the film's form, critics and public largely failed to grasp (perhaps mercifully) the acerbic mockery of its surreal satire, gut-reacting to its imagery as if it were intended as naively literal entertainment as opposed to a part satire of the concept. As a result, the stripshow sequence predictably engendered particular aversion, the *Daily Mirror* conceding that 'there were protests too, about a striptease scene, though no-one had grasped its meaning.'[62] Perhaps more surprisingly, critics also attacked the Beatles' soundtrack to the film, the *Daily Express* describing the songs as 'quite unmemorable'.[63]

Even when one considers the film's radical nature, it is truly amazing that it received such derogatory reactions from a press and public who had previously lauded the Beatles as the darlings of British pop culture. After all, although Ray Connolly suggests that critics were 'not yet ready to see their family favourites step over into the avant-garde',[64] both press and public had, as I have noted, been prepared to let the group experiment with new and frequently experimental fashions and musical forms prior to the film's conception. Faced with this evidence, one has to look beyond the form of the film and question whether there were any other direct or indirect factors which also contributed to its vituperative reception and commercial failure.

The answer to this is a resounding 'yes', and there are several factors which one could posit as contributing to the unfavourable reaction to the film. First, it must be said that, as a multi-media sales campaign which comprised a record and a film, *Magical Mystery Tour* was beset by organizational problems. Prior to its release, previous Beatles soundtrack albums had been released concurrently with their films, creating a dual hysteria and an anticipated build-up for their release. However, possibly sensing that the highly experimental nature of both the songs and the double EP package needed more time to 'catch' than their predecessors, NEMS sensibly planned to rush-release the EP on 1 December, four weeks before the film was due to be screened, allowing both audience and critics to build up a familiarity with the musical material.[65] However, two major problems affected this strategy from the outset. A hold-up in the printing of the colour booklet meant a delay of over a week[66] and, when the record was delivered to stores, dealers were confused by its unprecedented format. As a contemporary *Melody Maker* item reports, dealers had problems with marketing the release as they were 'not sure how to treat the record, because it isn't a conventional single or album'.[67] It was another week before the confusion was cleared, and the record was properly marketed as a single.

Yet while these factors can be attributed to bad luck, it must be said that the marketing of the release was unconventional to say the least. With their eye on the profitable Christmas number one slot, EMI had released a new Beatles single, 'Hello, Goodbye' just two weeks earlier, thus over-saturating the market with Beatles product, and restricting the potential air play of the *Magical Mystery Tour* material. There is considerable irony in the notion that the EP was at least partially denied the Christmas number one spot by another Beatles single. On top of this, the film and EP's centrepiece, 'I Am the Walrus' had, as I have noted, been banned from Radio 1 by the station's bosses. With the 'pirate' radio stations recently banned, the song had no alternative outlet of promotion. As a result of these developments, public and critics had been given less exposure to the soundtrack songs than they may have needed to appreciate the unconventional nature of the material. George Melly, writing about the film in *Revolt into Style*, believes that this was certainly central to the hostile reaction, maintaining that the songs were 'admirable' but that if they 'had had time to become familiar, the film might well have aroused less irritation'.[68]

Another possible reason for the public and critics' hostility could be the broadcasting slot allotted to the film. The film was screened at 8.35 p.m. on BBC1 at a time usually reserved for more conventional films or light entertainment. As we have established, *Magical Mystery Tour* did not fit into such a category, and its radical style would have seemed especially frustrating to a public who would naturally have expected something more conventional (even from the Beatles) at this time in the evening. As Peter Black of *The Listener* commented, 'Slotted into one of the arts programmes' times, the Beatles film would hardly have raised a whisper.'[69] However, there were significant reasons why this did not happen. First, the Beatles' music was, until *Magical Mystery Tour*, a phenomenon which, at least for the last two or three years, had appealed across ages, cultures and classes. Everything they produced created massive popular interest and although the film was a critical failure, it was watched by a huge audience of around twenty million viewers.[70] With such enormous public interest, the BBC would have been ill advised to give it anything other than a prime-time slot. Moreover, apart from being given an aesthetically unsuitable slot, the film was also first broadcast in black and white, and as Gavrik Losey rightly maintains, 'It had to be seen in colour to make any sense at all.'[71] Indeed, although the reason for this decision has never been fully revealed, there is no doubt that it was completely insensitive to the brightly coloured psychedelic aesthetic of such sequences as the 'Flying' extravaganza. Devoid of its startling colour-filtered effects, the entire *raison d'être* of its aesthetic and meaning is completely undermined.

Finally, there is another important yet totally external factor which could possibly have contributed to the film's negative reception, this being the timing of the hostile reaction which greeted McCartney's public admission that he had taken LSD and endorsed the experience. In June 1967, articles in *Queen* magazine in Britain and *Life* in America featured interviews with McCartney in which he admitted having used the drug and included comments regarding the possibilities of LSD as a universal cure for social evils. Here, McCartney explained that LSD had opened his eyes to a greater understanding of the human condition, claiming that 'we only use one tenth of our brain. Just think of all that we could accomplish if we could only tap that hidden part. It would mean a whole new world. If the politicians would take LSD, there wouldn't be any more war, or poverty or famine.'[72] Whether or not his comments were intended to promote sensationalist controversy, or whether he just wanted to use his cultural influence to popularize a substance which he personally endorsed at the time, is a debatable issue. However, according to Peter Brown, director of NEMS, the statement was made in a 'moment of unsurpassed folly',[73] causing a storm of outrage when discovered by the British press and making the previously 'wholesome' Beatles for a time personally unpopular, not only with most of the disapproving press, but also with mainstream youth magazines such as *Melody Maker*.

When Epstein (previously regarded as Britain's most admirable and exemplary impresario) had leapt to McCartney's defence and maintained that he also endorsed the drug, the controversy ballooned to new proportions, with both group and manager caught in a crossfire of public scorn. Epstein was 'widely criticized in newspaper editorials, TV commentaries, and by parent and church groups for his confession. It was discussed at length on the floor of the House of Commons, and the Home Office released an official statement saying that it was "horrified" at Epstein's attitude towards this dangerous drug.'[74] The LSD incident, which mirrored Lennon's 1966 faux-pas about being 'bigger than Jesus',[75] changed consensus attitudes towards the Beatles. Their music (which had, at least on a populist level, long been considered as 'beyond reproach') was still universally loved and adored (and bought!), but while the admission helped to clarify their godhead status within factions of the underground (who also presumably loved the film), it did little for their larger, and more 'mainstream', following. Indeed, while most of the press and public were prepared to enjoy a superficial appreciation of the fashions and music of 'flower power', it is clear that their fundamental conservatism meant that they were largely unprepared to accept the more serious ramifications of a flourishing drug culture. Singles releases notwithstanding, the group's next major project after the LSD furore was *Magical Mystery Tour*.[76] Although it is impossible to garner any concrete evidence that the press reaction to the film was coloured by any sense of moral 'revenge', it is clearly an interesting possibility. What is certain is that *Magical Mystery Tour*, with its combination of blatantly drug-induced imagery, simulated 'trips' and vérité footage of a frequently 'stoned' looking group, could not, in the light of these developments, have been timed more badly.

Notes

1. Figure supplied by Denis O'Dell, interviewed by author, 30 April 1996.
2. Miles, 1978, p. 107.
3. Connolly, 1981, p. 85.
4. Their use of LSD has been widely discussed. See, for example, Hertsgaard, 1995, pp. 191–200.
5. The Beatles' backing of the underground press was consistent throughout the late sixties. They frequently gave exclusive interviews to magazines such as *Oz* and *IT*, and occasionally donated much needed finances. See, for example, *The Paul McCartney World Tour*, tour brochure, 1989, and Hutchinson, 1992, p. 97.
6. The Beatles' first serious flirtation with transcendental meditation occurred in August 1967, when they visited their guru, the Maharishi Mahesh Yogi, in Bangor, Wales. It was here that they learned of Epstein's death.
7. Lennon reveals this in a seventies television interview (title unknown) featured in the film documentary, *Imagine* (Warner Bros, 1988).
8. Joe McGrath, interviewed by author, 13 February 1996.
9. The album was the first Beatles release to sustain a chart run of over one hundred weeks.
10. 'Beatles News November 1967', *Beatles Monthly Book*, no. 140, December 1987, p. 12.
11. Hutchinson, 1992, p. 41.
12. Blake was involved in the *Sergeant Pepper* album cover; Hamilton designed the cover for *The Beatles* (1968) album.

13. McCartney discusses his associations with the mid to late sixties avant-garde in *The Paul McCartney World Tour*, tour brochure, 1989, pp. 50–1. See also Bennahum, 1991, p. 92.
14. Evans, 1984, p. 94.
15. Booker, 1970, p. 240.
16. 'London: the Swinging City', *Time*, vol.87, no.15, 1966, p. 32.
17. Barrow, 1987a, p. 5.
18. Victor Spinetti, interviewed by author, 29 April 1996.
19. Gavrik Losey, intervewed by author, 27 March 1996.
20. Documented in a number of sources. See, for example, Norman, 1981, p. 311.
21. Price taken from Lewisohn, 1989, p. 131.
22. See, for example, Norman, 1981, p. 310.
23. Denis O'Dell, interviewed by author.
24. Miles, 1978, p. 111.
25. Gambaccini, 1976, p. 48.
26. Wenner, 1973, p. 76.
27. *Imagine* (Warner Bros, 1988).
28. Victor Spinetti, interviewed by author.
29. According to Lewisohn, 1992, p. 273, the final *Top of the Pops* airing of the song (Christmas Day, 1968) completely negated all these combinations, opting instead for BBC footage of a London/Brighton train journey.
30. Walker, 1986, p. 226.
31. Joe McGrath, interviewed by author.
32. Miles, 1978, p. 111.
33. MacDonald, 1995, p. 204.
34. Mid to late sixties youth culture comprised a vast range of underground sub-cultures informed by a number of different utopian ideals. These ideals encompassed drug culture (and particularly LSD), humanitarian causes such as CND, predominantly Eastern religious orders such as Zen Buddhism and Sufism, together with strands of political activity (such as the British 'New Left'). Much British counter-culture was based upon imported ideas from American and Indian gurus, leaders and activists such as Timothy Leary, Alan Watts and the Maharishi Mahesh Yogi. The so-called 'underground' became the buzzword for alternative lifestyles, which were popularized and discussed in Britain in publications such as *IT* (est. 1966) and *Oz* (est. 1967). For an expansive study of sixties counter-culture, see Leech, 1973. Although different factions were frequently ideologically opposed (for example, the doctrines of Zen Buddhism are fundamentally opposed to drug culture), they were united by a deep distrust of dominant lifestyles and the moral values of capitalism, state authority and the nuclear family upon which Western society is built. Moreover, the various 'alternative' modes of belief and perception, whether political, humanist, spiritual or drug-oriented, shared a fundamental interest in ideas understood to be either consciousness-raising or expanding.
35. Kureishi, 1991, p. 88.
36. MacDonald, 1994, pp. 213–14.
37. Making alternative forms of entertainment was an integral part of underground culture, although the adjectives 'free' and 'spontaneous' are often misleading since 'happenings' had to be planned and financed like any conventional entertainment. According to Neville, 1970, pp. 24–7, the 'seeds of London's first psychedelic circus' were planted in June 1965 with Allen Ginsberg's famous 'Cosmic Poetry Visitation

Accidentally Happening Carnally' event at the Albert Hall. By 1967, 'happenings' such as psychedelic concerts (often accompanied by 'hallucinatory' light shows) took off in such fashionable nightspots as London's UFO Club and The Electric Garden, a haven for the newly emerging music of artists such as Pink Floyd and Arthur Brown.

38. Marwick, 1990, p. 125.
39. Denis O'Dell, interviewed by author.
40. Ibid.
41. Evans, 1984, p. 78.
42. Although *Sergeant Pepper* crystallized the Beatles' psychedelic influences, *Revolver* contains the seedlings of drug-induced inspiration, particularly in the acid-inspired songs 'Tommorrow Never Knows' and 'She Said She Said', widely known by fans to have been derived from an encounter between Lennon and a tripping Peter Fonda.
43. Evans, 1984, p. 76.
44. Spence, 1981, p. 84.
45. Norman, 1981, p. 306.
46. 'The Fool' were a primarily Dutch design team who became heavily involved with the Beatles around the time of *Magical Mystery Tour*. They were commissioned (for £100,000) to design hippy attire for the Apple boutique, and also created the psychedelic costumes for the Beatles' appearance on the *Our World* television special.
47. Melly, 1970, p. 106.
48. Evans and Aspinall, 1967, p. 8.
49. Norman, 1981, p. 313.
50. Kenelm Jenour, 'Beatles' Mystery Tour Baffles Viewers', *Daily Mirror*, 27 December 1967.
51. Ibid.
52. *Melody Maker*, 6 January 1968, p. 16.
53. It did, however, later receive limited theatrical screenings in Los Angeles and San Francisco. According to

Harry, 1984, p. 66, these took place in May 1968.
54. Ibid.
55. Figure from Brown and Gaines, 1984, p. 244.
56. Although also a speedy seller (according to Lewisohn, 1989, p. 131, the record sold half a million copies before the film was released at Christmas), the EP failed to repeat the previous success of such million-selling singles as 'She Loves You', 'I Want to Hold Your Hand', 'Can't Buy Me Love', 'I Feel Fine', 'We Can Work It Out/ Day Tripper'.
57. Don Short, 'So We Boobed Says Beatle Paul', *Daily Mirror*, 28 December 1967.
58. James Thomas, 'Magic Leaves Beatles with Mighty Flop', *Daily Express*, 27 December 1967.
59. Ibid. Thomas concluded that the Beatles were 'four rather pleasant young men who have made so much money that they can apparently afford to be contemptuous of the public'.
60. Robin Turner, 'Even Beethoven Wasn't Great All the Time', *Daily Express*, 28 December 1967.
61. Don Short, 'So We Boobed Says Beatle Paul', *Daily Mirror*, 28 December 1967.
62. Kenelm Jenour, 'Beatles' Mystery Tour Baffles Viewers', *Daily Mirror*, 27 December 1967.
63. James Thomas, 'Magic Leaves Beatles with Mighty Flop', *Daily Express*, 27 December 1967.
64. Connolly, 1981, p. 89.
65. 'Beatle News', *Beatles Monthly Book*, no.54, January 1968, p. 29.
66. Ibid.
67. *Melody Maker*, 9 December 1967.
68. Melly, 1970, p. 178.
69. Peter Black, 'Nay, Nay, Nay', *The Listener*, vol. 79, no. 2023, 4 January 1968, p. 27.

70. Figure given by Paul Fox, head of BBC1, in Robin Turner, 'Even Beethoven Wasn't Great All the Time', *Daily Express*, 28 December 1967.
71. Gavrik Losey, interviewed by author.
72. Thompson, 1967, p. 105.
73. Brown and Gaines, 1984, p. 218.
74. Ibid., p. 219.
75. Lennon's remarks regarding Christianity, made to Maureen Cleave of the *London Evening Standard*, caused enormous controversy in the US when published in a teenage magazine titled *Datebook*. Reactions were particularly vehement in the southern states of America where Beatles records were ritually burnt. When arriving in America for the US leg of their 1966 tour, Lennon publicly apologized for his remark.
76. Shortly after his comments were published, McCartney stressed that he had not wished to advocate the use of LSD, and blamed the media for being irresponsible. However, despite this, and subsequent announcements that the group had given up drugs, the stigma, like the influence of mind-expanding substances, did not disappear so easily.

4

Sergeant Pepper Goes to the Movies:
Yellow Submarine

Of all the official Beatles movies of the sixties, the animated feature, *Yellow Submarine*, is perhaps the one with the strangest production genesis. Unlike their previous television feature, the Beatles personally had very little involvement in its production history. However, the labyrinthine twists and turns that led to the film's eventual production pre-date the *Magical Mystery Tour* episode by a considerable period, and to trace the film's origins we must briefly backtrack to 1964.

During that year, Epstein had been approached by an ambitious Hungarian-American cartoon producer, Al Brodax, whose company, King Features, had been responsible for the evergreen *Popeye* series. With the outbreak of Beatlemania, Brodax wanted to produce an American cartoon series starring the group and their songs. Epstein, although slightly reluctant to have his increasingly stoical assets trivialized into cartoon characters, saw no far-reaching or harmful consequences in the venture and struck a deal with Brodax. Thus began, in September 1965, a series of cartoon shorts starring the group in around sixty short animated adventures in which the 'moptop' Beatles were chased around (*Help!*-style) by an assortment of weird and wonderful characters and fans. The series, which based its episode titles on their songs, was networked on US television by ABC, but not shown on British television until much later, and then only in one TV region.[1] Despite this, it proved extremely popular internationally, eventually running for two years and earning the Beatles and Epstein 50 per cent of the project's profits.[2]

In their initial dealings Epstein had promised Brodax the group's cooperation for a feature film if the series turned out to be successful. In 1966, Brodax reminded Epstein of his promise and succeeded in getting him to agree to endorse the project with the Beatles' names and four new original songs for the soundtrack. Neither Epstein nor the Beatles had been particularly keen on the idea but, according to McCabe and Schonfeld, they saw the film as 'a means of fulfilling their obligation to provide United Artists with a third film'.[3] This, as we shall see in the next chapter, turned out to be a misplaced judgement.

Production began in 1967 and was initially envisaged by Brodax to be a kind of *Fantasia*-style production which, like the cartoon series, would be heavily based on the imagery and allusions of the group's contemporary recordings. As Brodax later commented, 'We derived a lot from the *Sergeant Pepper* album. We took the word "pepper", which is positive, spicy, and created a place called Pepperland which is full of colour and music. But in the hills around live Blue Meanies, who hate colour, hate everything positive.'[4] The production itself was financed by Brodax's American company and produced (for $1million[5]) through TVC (TV Cartoons) in London. The director was the Canadian animator, George Dunning, and the writing credits were shared by Brodax, Lee Minoff, Jack Mendelsohn and Erich Segal, a professor of Greek and Latin at Yale, who later wrote the hugely successful *Love Story* (1970). In some ways, the employment of Dunning as director mirrored that of Lester some years earlier for *A Hard Day's Night* and *Help!* Like Lester, Dunning had worked in commercials during the fifties and, again like the American director, his approach to film-making married commercial instinct with avant-garde sensibilities. As well as having worked on avant-garde shorts like *Cadet Rouselle* (1945), Dunning had also gained invaluable experience with more commercial ventures (in the early fifties he had worked in America at UPA on *The Gerald McBoing Boing Show*), and by the time he moved to London and set up TVC in 1956 his experience and aptitude for stylistic breadth took in a breathtaking range of influences derived from experience gleaned from living and working in Canada, Paris and America. Five years before *Yellow Submarine*, his short film *The Flying Man* (1962) had won the Grand Prix at the Annecy International Animation Festival.

The fantasy story of the feature was based on an idea by Lee Minoff, in turn derived from the Lennon and McCartney title track which, as well as appearing as one half of the highly successful 'Eleanor Rigby' double A-side single, was also a hugely popular album track from the 1966 album release, *Revolver*. Although the Beatles were not closely involved with the making of the film, which included work by two hundred animators worldwide, McCartney gave his blessing to Minoff's first screenplay outline which, according to Lewisohn, is dated November 1966 and states the following objective: 'The goal should be nothing less than to take animation beyond anything seen before in style, class and tone, but avoiding the precious and pretentious.'[6] However, achieving this objective proved no small task and, according to actor Paul Angelis, the script underwent fourteen re-writes before it was finally completed.[7] Moreover, it has been suggested that other uncredited writers were involved in the project, most notably Roger McGough, the Mersey poet and member of the pop group the Scaffold, who, according to Angelis, 'wrote a lot of the Beatles' dialogue'.[8]

What is certain is that neither Apple nor the Beatles had much involvement in the film's production. Indeed, although the film credits state the film to be an Apple Presentation (which Denis O'Dell negotiated to 'make it more official',[9]) the Beatles' contribution was limited to the four contractually enforced original songs, a few minor script ideas, and a brief appearance at the film's closure, again negotiated by O'Dell, who also tried (albeit unsuccessfully) to get the Beatles to lend their own voices to the project.[10] In the end, the Beatles' voices were dubbed by actors and even the idea of producing four original songs was treated with marginal disdain by the group. As George Martin explains, 'Their reaction was, "OK, we've got to supply them with these bloody songs, but we're not going to fall over backwards providing them. We'll let them have them whenever we feel like it, and we'll give them whatever we think is all right."'[11] In the event, the Beatles grudgingly honoured Epstein's commitment and provided the film soundtrack with four new numbers, 'It's All Too Much', 'Only a Northern Song', 'Hey Bulldog' and 'All Together Now'. While I shall discuss later what I consider to be the frequently overlooked merits of this material, it must be conceded that the songs were, at least in part, culled from sources external to the film itself. The second number (a Harrison composition) had been a left-over from the *Sergeant Pepper* LP, and 'It's All Too Much', another Harrison number, dated from May 1967. However, although the group were initially sceptical about the film, thinking that it would put their newly acquired 'intellectual' image back several years, they had a massive change of heart when they saw the film in its almost finished state and were, in

Barrow's words, 'So pleased with the way the whole production had been put together that they were only too happy to associate themselves with it more closely from then on.'[12]

Formally, the film is rooted in a range of sixties pop styles, and the eclecticism of its colour imagery (designed largely by German poster artist Heinz Edelmann) is derived from a vast range of popular contemporary styles, including imagery culled from the pop art paintings, prints and designs of artists such as Peter Blake and Andy Warhol, the 'op' art of Bridget Riley, surrealist and expressionist art, the psychedelic graphics of British and American underground poster designers such as Martin Sharp and Rick Griffin, and the work of popular illustrators such as Alan Aldridge, who was apparently initially involved with creating some of the draft drawings for the animation.[13] Looking at *Yellow Submarine* with the benefit of almost thirty years hindsight, the cutting-edge, contemporaneous, 'now' aesthetic of its imagery inevitably makes it appear as something of a museum piece to the modern eye, yet in its day the animation was accurately described by Joel W. Finler as a 'remarkable summation and integration of the best in British and American pop design of the sixties'.[14]

Considering the imagery and allusions of the Beatles' music of this period, it is perhaps unsurprising that one of the most pronounced styles to be absorbed into the film's animation is that of British and American psychedelic poster art. In the mid-sixties, the cheap disposability of affordable, mass-produced psychedelic posters became heavily absorbed into pop culture through the work of such artists as Nigel Waymouth (of 'Haphash') and Martin Sharp, one of the key designers of *Oz*. Although such a-commercial posters and magazine pullouts sometimes had quasi-political or overtly propagandist purposes (such as 'Legalize Pot' or 'Plant a Flower Child'), their central purpose seemed to be more concerned with celebrating, through a combination of photo-montage, reworked fine art and original cartoon-style graphics, the spiritual benefits of different kinds of mind expansion, their hallucinatory aesthetic obviating the need for their copious colourful typography to be totally legible or conventionally 'understandable'. The psychedelic poster art of the aforementioned designers (and indeed the literary illustrations of Alan Aldridge and the psychedelic photography of Richard Avedon[15]) popularized the use of bright primary colours and surreal imagery derived from the urge to produce art which simulated the LSD experience. The animation style of *Yellow Submarine* is also heavily influenced by the psychedelic aesthetic and, beyond the story itself, the film boasts iconography which, in its use of colour and patently psychedelic imagery, mimics that of the underground press and American West Coast poster design. Perhaps the best example of this can be seen in the simulated 'trip' sequence which accompanies Harrison's 'Only a Northern Song'. Here, bright strobes of alternating primary colour and close-ups of the Beatles' ears attached to frequency monitors emphasize a higher reality than that of the objective world and, in the employment of irrational imagery and a visceral onslaught of 'mind-blowing' colour, attempt to simulate a hypnotic 'psych-out' of epic proportions.

Like psychedelic poster art, the animation also invests in elaborate and fluorescent 'Disney-style' typography, although unlike so many West Coast designs, the lettering is never so elaborately transformed that it becomes illegible. Although often hypnotically multiplied *à la* Warhol, the lettering never ceases to have an implicitly rational meaning within the narrative's fantasy discourse. Indeed, so important is the meaning of lettering within the narrative that it actually becomes integrated causally into the dramatic action. Such is the case in the 'All You Need Is Love' sequence towards the end, when the terrifying and deadly 'Glove' is kept at bay by John, who physically bombards it with the word 'Love' whilst simultaneously delivering the song.

The film's iconography also shares psychedelic art's nostalgic celebration of all things Edwardian. Indeed, just as the sinewy art nouveau imagery of Aubrey Beardsley became integrated into many designers' work (see, for example, Martin Sharp's Bob Dylan poster of 1967, 'Blowing in the Mind'), so it finds its place in *Yellow Submarine*, and it is interesting to note that the inhabitants of Pepperland (grandfathers on penny-farthings, servants, maids and colourfully uniformed soldiers) are almost uniformly pseudo-Edwardian in appearance. Indeed, what could be more fundamentally Edwardian than *Sergeant Pepper's Lonely Hearts Club Band* itself? Interestingly, much of the Beatles' music from this period was also deeply rooted in a desire for historical pastiche. While songs such as 'When I'm Sixty Four' were, as we noted in the last chapter, essentially attempts to recreate the atmosphere of the music hall, 'Being for the Benefit of Mr Kite', for all its psychedelic allusions, is fundamentally

Victorian in essence, inspired as it was by a real Victorian circus poster picked up at an antiques shop in Kent by Lennon. As George Melly maintains in *Revolt into Style*, 'Alone in pop, with the possible exception of the Kinks, the Beatles are at their happiest when celebrating the past. They display little enthusiasm for the way we live now.'[16]

Elsewhere, the film integrates the styles of other forms of popular posters and contemporary pop art, most specifically through the fascination with famous images of icons from contemporary and historical stage, screen and comic-book art. Indeed, while the images of non-psychedelic contemporary poster art employed huge blow-ups of such vintage icons as Charlie Chaplin, Humphrey Bogart and Laurel and Hardy, the pop art paintings and graphic designs of Peter Blake and the screen prints of Andy Warhol became preoccupied with images of contemporary stars such as Elvis Presley and the Beatles themselves. These contemporary obsessions are constantly present in *Yellow Submarine*, although perhaps the best example is the sequence in which Ringo and Old Fred are searching for the other Beatles and move into a vast anti-chamber populated solely by historical figures (General Custer), screen stars (Monroe, Astaire), and comic-book heroes. Tellingly, their collage-style presentation closely resembles Blake's layout for that most enduring image of sixties pop graphics, the Beatles' *Sergeant Pepper* cover.

Finally, the film also manages to employ imagery from a number of more exclusively 'fine' art disciplines, and the influence of Warhol's pop art is never far away. However, perhaps the most obvious homage to his style is present in the extraordinary 'Eleanor Rigby' sequence and, although the sad characters which populate the desolate Liverpool cityscape are the thematic antithesis of his own glamorous subjects, their execution bears startling iconographical and textural resemblance to his mid to late sixties polymer paint and silk screen prints. Equally obvious is the influence of Bridget Riley's op art; the bedazzling black-and-white imagery in the 'Sea of Holes' sequence shares the same disorienting geometric distortion of space and perspective as much of her playful mid-sixties work. Elsewhere, the film also manages to integrate images from less contemporary art. Indeed, while the semi-abstract colours and shapes of the 'Lucy in the Sky with Diamonds' sequence might be tentatively described as a kind of animated

8) 'I Am the Walrus'. The Beatles shooting *Magical Mystery Tour*.
©Apple Corps Ltd.

9) Masters of pastiche: 'Your Mother Should Know'. ©Apple Corps Ltd.

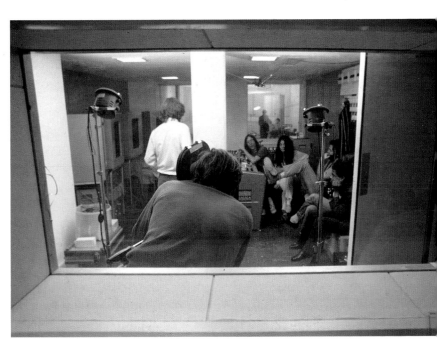

10) Shooting *Let It Be*. ©Apple Corps Ltd.

11) *Magical Mystery Tour.* ©Apple Corps Ltd.

12) Passing the audition: The final concert for *Let It Be*. ©Apple Corps Ltd.

Kandinsky on acid, the pulsing, melting clocks which appear in the 'Sea of Time' scenes are directly lifted from Dali's *Persistence of Memory* (1931).

In his astonishing survey of pop art culture, George Melly analyses the eclectic form of sixties iconography. In his discussion of psychedelic poster art (and specifically the notorious 'Haphash' design group) he draws the following conclusion:

> ... when it comes to imagery there is no attempt to conceal a magpie approach to any artist past or present who seems to strike the right psychedelic note. As a result the 'Haphash' posters are almost a collage of other men's hard-won visions: Mucha, Ernst, Magritte, Bosch, William Blake, comic books, engravings of Red Indians, Disney, Dulac, ancient illustrations of treatises on alchemy; everything is boiled down to make a visionary and hallucinatory bouillabaisse.[17]

He could have been discussing the visual approach of *Yellow Submarine*. Although, as we have seen, the film occasionally absorbs its imagery from different sources, the iconoclastic approach to imagery is fundamentally identical. Not only does the film absorb the inherent and exclusive properties of psychedelic art, it also applies the same selectively eclectic approach, and it is clearly no coincidence that the styles which it tends to absorb (particularly surrealism and op) are fundamentally implicitly 'hallucinatory' by nature. They do indeed strike the 'right note'.

Beyond its imagery, it is perhaps also productive to apply this theory to the highly eclectic methods of animation technique, which comprise conventional cel animation, rotoscoping (the technique of simulating animated drawings over live-action sequences), and conventional live-action sequences (the final sequence where the real Beatles make a fleeting guest appearance). Although alternating between the first two techniques was not especially new to animated features (it had been used in Disney films since the thirties), *Yellow Submarine* integrates these styles simultaneously rather than interchangeably, using them together to create the disorienting 'trippiness' for which the film has become justly renowned.[18]

If the film's form is heavily influenced by psychedelic principles, then so too is the narrative, albeit in a more subtle manner than in *Magical*

Mystery Tour. Indeed, the cleverness of the story, which pits the Beatles (and/or their alter egos of Sergeant Pepper's Lonely Hearts Club Band) against the despicable Blue Meanies, is that it is seemingly constructed to be interpretable (to different factions of the audience) on many levels. On one hand, it can be read as a simple, nostalgic children's/family fantasy tale of the forces of good versus the forces of darkness, and, on the other, as an underground parable of how the psychedelic Beatles (symbols of the peaceful and apolitical forces of hippy counter-culture) overcome the forces of state power to establish a new regime of karmic awareness and universal goodwill. In short, the narrative rewards the audience with the limit of its own experience. It is worth considering this second interpretation in greater detail to assess what, beyond the use of the visual style, the narrative had to offer to the underground.

Firstly, the very title of the film held hidden significance for the flourishing drug culture, since a 'Yellow Submarine' (or 'Yellow Sub') was also the elaborate title ascribed to a brand of popular narcotic pill for 'heads'. Although the Beatles have always denied any 'hidden meanings' and claimed it to be nothing more than a 'children's song',[19] it is not unreasonable to question such a simplistic explanation. While their claims would to some degree seem to be consolidated by the use of Starr (the 'children's favourite') as lead vocalist, the identical titles would suggest there is more to the song than meets the ear and, whatever the Beatles' intentions, there is no denying that the song title had loaded implications for some of the audience. Secondly, the film's travelogue narrative, which to children and 'unenlightened' adults is merely an 'innocent' surreal fantasy voyage, is, to underground converts, a simulated hallucinatory 'trip' which, developing the themes of *Magical Mystery Tour*, seems intent on conveying the viewer from one acid-soaked vision of the mind's eye to the next. As the cartoon Beatles repeatedly and knowingly maintain, the world they inhabit is 'all in the mind'.

Within this world live the wicked Blue Meanies, who can be read as simplistic symbols of the ultimate grassroots manifestation of state power, the police. Like the police, they carry weapons, wear blue uniforms, and use ferocious dogs. Revealingly, they remind Paul of another authority figure, his old English teacher. The heroic Beatles, who with their kindly goodwill and affable humour are presented as the antithesis of these characters, speak a self-referential language which is riddled with sly acknowledgements to their most heavily psychedelic songs, including the then recently banned 'A Day in the Life', 'Fixing a Hole', and 'With a Little Help from My Friends'. Indeed, while their dialogue contains drug-oriented references and 'in' jokes ('What day is it?' 'Sitarday.') which could not possibly have had any meaning for a juvenile audience, the chosen soundtrack songs (largely culled from *Sergeant Pepper*) are also almost always those which possess the largest quota of drug-oriented imagery. Whatever Lennon may have subsequently said about the lyrical content of 'Lucy in the Sky with Diamonds' (and I see no reason to disbelieve the oft-repeated story of his young son's drawing acting as lyrical inspiration[20]), there is no doubt that it offers itself to be read as a psychedelic 'trip' song, bursting with paranoic tension and sinister metamorphic iconography. Indeed, even the more overtly 'innocent' and 'unenlightened' non-'Pepper' soundtrack songs contain lyrics which can be deciphered to suggest double meanings and references to alternative lifestyles. Such is the case in McCartney's 'All Together Now', which, with its lyrical marriage of childlike, nursery rhyme naivety and risque references to promiscuity, creates an ambiguity which could only have been intentional.

The final narrative equilibrium, in which the Beatles' defeat of the Blue Meanies restores the harmonious karmic order of Pepperland, is also open to an 'underground' reading, although not perhaps one which would have been so universally welcomed by its more radical and politicized factions, who, by 1968 and the film's release, were beginning to feel that the group's 'flower power' philosophies of meditation, drugs, love and peace ('inner' revolution) were no longer a viable substitute for 'outward' protest and occasionally 'justified' violent activism.[21] Indeed, in many ways the presentation of the Beatles' spiritual vision of counter-culture is, for all its Leary-like undertones, essentially closer to the more populist 'alternative' doctrines of Christianity or Hinduism (central to different strands of counter-culture during 1967) than to certain transatlantic and European strands of the movement which, since the Tet offensive of February 1968 in Vietnam and the French student uprising (May 1968) were becoming increasingly absorbed into strands of Trotskyism, Maoism and anarchism. While such militant factions would possibly have welcomed the fact that the Beatles, in *Yellow Submarine*, instigate a symbolic social revolution by establishing a new world order in Pepperland, it is clearly symptomatic of both the film's 1967 genesis and the Beatles' unwillingness to relinquish their advocacy of 1967's peace-oriented philosophies, that the 'revolution' is achieved more through the redemptive consciousness-raising powers of music and nature than by violent retribution. Significantly, the group's 'army' can only ultimately 'defeat' the Meanies by changing their ideals, and this is achieved by magically making flowers spring up on to their bodies, literally equating the forces of revolution and change with 'flower power'.

Indeed, it is tempting to suggest that *Yellow Submarine* is the cinematic cousin of one of the most famous and enduring images of hippy counter-culture, the photograph of the flower being inserted into the barrel of a gun. At no point in the film do the Beatles take punitive action against the Meanies; they merely want to re-establish the utopian peace of Pepperland. While a brutal resolution would obviously have been unsuitable for a family audience (and therefore in direct opposition to the film's populist commercial aspirations), it is clearly salient that the revolution is, to quote MacDonald's well-chosen book title, 'in the head'. In essence, then, the underlying message of the film's climax (that love conquers everything) is not dissimilar to Lennon's controversial message to disaffected sixties youth, 'Revolution 1', recorded for *The Beatles* (aka *The White Album*) in the month of the film's release: do not exchange the principles of love and spirituality for violent retribution – real change can only be instigated by the shifting of consciousness.[22] In this sense the film perfectly mirrors the holistic ideas which pervaded many of the other, more overtly spiritual and psychedelic songs of the 1967/68 period. Indeed, it is perhaps no coincidence that Lennon's stirring and sentimental 'All You Need Is Love' was later deployed to pad out the soundtrack LP: besides its spiritual themes of anti-materialism, temperance and tolerance, the title itself forms as neat a poetic summation of the film's ideology as one is likely to find.

Although their involvement in the film was small, *Yellow Submarine* crystallized the real Beatles vision of counter-culture with a dexterity and accessibility that far surpassed that of *Magical Mystery Tour*. With the possible exception of the 'militant' youth, it really was 'all-inclusive' in its attempt to attain cross-cultural appeal, and its projected vision of a utopian hippydom subtle enough to appeal only to those who searched for or expected it. With its undertones of pacifism and spirituality, it was fundamentally populistic enough to be acceptable to those adults who found the more radical and militant ideals of the underground's more materialist strands to be objectionable or threatening. Indeed, as *Variety* wisely noted upon the film's release, 'The pic should be a sure click with Beatles' fans and youthful "pop" audiences and also intrigue those who sometimes tut tut the remarkable combo's more wayout activities.'[23]

The film was premiered at the London Pavilion on 17 July 1968. Again the Beatles attended personally and the traffic around Piccadilly Circus once more came to a standstill as thousands of fans swarmed across central London. Outside the theatre, costumed characters from the film entertained the crowds, and fans also caught glimpses of contemporary celebrities, including members of the Rolling Stones and Cream, James Taylor and Twiggy. All had been requested by the group to wear something yellow, and after the screening around 200 VIP guests made their way to the Royal Lancaster Hotel on Bayswater Road, where the hotel's newly built disco, 'The Yellow Submarine', had just opened.

The film was of course accompanied by a soundtrack album, although there were two important differences from the Beatles' other film-oriented material. First, it was the first British-issued film soundtrack album to include material which was not performed or written by the group. Although side one of the LP comprised the four 'new' songs mentioned earlier (plus the previously released title track and 'All You Need Is Love'), the second side contained nothing but extracts from George Martin's powerful instrumental score. Secondly, the album was not concurrently released with the film; it was released on 13 January 1969, seven months after the premiere, possibly because the group felt that the film soundtrack should not coincide with their most ambitious *White Album* project, which was released in Britain on 22 November 1968. On a more practical level, Mark Lewisohn, in his authoratitive *Complete Beatles Recording Sessions*, notes that George Martin wanted to re-record his instrumental side of the album, which he did (with the aid of a forty-one piece orchestra) in two three-hour sessions at Abbey Road on 22 and 23 October 1968.[24]

The critics were by and large kind to the film, their reception in marked contrast to the venomous response which greeted *Magical Mystery Tour* just seven months earlier. However, before they had actually seen the film, many reviewers were no more enamoured of the idea of a full-length cartoon film than the group themselves. Indeed, just three days after the first broadcast of *Magical Mystery Tour*, the *Daily Mail* ran an article titled 'After That Flop the Cartoon Beatles', which complained that 'the Beatles stubbornly continue to experiment'.[25] Despite these fears, the film received generally positive reviews. The tabloids were generally ecstatic, with the *Daily Mail's* Cecil Wilson running a headline which simply stated 'Dazzled by That Yellow Submarine', his review enthusiastically comparing the character of Jeremy Hilary Boob (the 'Nowhere Man') with Disney characters.[26] The quality press were also impressed, with reviews from Patrick Gibb and John Russell Taylor respectively describing the film as 'brilliantly inventive' and proudly announcing the arrival of 'a British cartoon film that's sure to please everyone'.[27] Nigel Gosling of the *Observer* was also enthusiastic, maintaining that the film 'packs in more stimulation, sly art-references and pure joy into ninety minutes than a mile of exhibitions of op and pop and all the mod cons'.[28] Specialist film magazines were no less enthralled, with Gavin Millar of *Sight and Sound* picking up on the scope of the film's formal eclecticism and describing it as both a 'pleasure and surprise'.[29] More importantly for the Beatles' underground following, Joel W. Finler of *IT* also gave the film a very favourable notice.[30] However, there were some minor complaints about the film's drug-induced imagery in certain British and American publications. While *Esquire* referred to the iconography as an 'LSD zoo',[31] Felix Barker of the *Evening News* wrote an extremely scathing piece which maintained that 'you won't be able to get near the box office for hippies, flower people, Beatle-crushers, love-inners and sit-downers. And in every ten thousand teenagers, one elderly person of over twenty-five will join in vaguely hoping to keep with it. Others I predict will hate every five thousand two hundred and twenty seconds of this cartoon.'[32] Fortunately for the Beatles, Felix Barker was wrong, although this did not stop the film from undergoing some very unfortunate complications in Britain.

Although the film was a critical triumph, its potential commercial success in Britain was hampered by problems of exhibition. Rank, the film's British exhibitors, refused to screen the movie at all their 200 cinemas; contemporary reports show that the film was dropped from about half their outlets shortly after its release. On 6 August 1968 the

Daily Express ran an article titled 'Beatles Yellow Submarine Dropped by Cinemas', in which a spokesman for Rank maintained that the film's takings in the first three weeks of exhibition had been lower than expected and it would therefore receive only a limited release.[33] According to Bill Harry, the box-office receipts showed that this had been a miscalculation by Rank, but by then 'the damage had been done and Rank's decision to withdraw the film from more than half of their cinemas drastically affected its potential box office income in Britain'.[34] Despite this setback, the film is still regarded by Peter Brown and Steven Gaines as a commercial success[35] and, as Bill Harry notes, no such problems occurred with the American release, where the cartoon did exceptionally good business.[36]

However, the soundtrack album shifted fewer units than previous Beatle albums, no doubt because of its delayed release and lack of original material. Indeed, as Mark Lewisohn maintains, the Beatles were 'mildly criticized'[37] at the time for providing fans with less than their usual good value, and for the first time in Britain an 'original' Beatles album failed to make the number one spot, peaking at number three in the *Record Retailer* charts and faring little better in America. Interestingly, Lewisohn notes that the group probably also felt that fans had been somewhat 'cheated' by the lack of original material on the album release, noting that the EMI library contains a master tape for a seven-inch mono EP of the group's four original compositions for the film (plus an early mix of Lennon's haunting 'Across the Universe') which dates back to 13 March 1969.[38] This 33$\frac{1}{3}$ rpm EP, which was no doubt intended to restore goodwill amongst fans was of course never released, and Lewisohn suggests that the group, who weren't particularly pleased with their musical contribution to the film, simply decided upon 'washing their hands of the whole affair'.[39]

Yet despite the Beatles' relative unhappiness and ambivalent attitude to their musical numbers for the film's score, there can be no doubting its quality. Although the *Yellow Submarine* album was much criticized by fans for its poor value, George Martin's soundtrack still retains an extraordinary freshness and, whatever their production history, the Beatles' contributions to the record are never less than first-class. Indeed, although fans had every right to complain about the inclusion of two pre-released numbers, the two Harrison numbers alone are worth the admission price. Although continually disregarded by the majority of critics, 'It's All Too Much' must surely be the most underrated song in the Beatles' psychedelic canon. With its extraordinary tape loops and dense barrage of background effects, the song's production took the psychedelic aesthetic to its logical conclusion, and the integration of classical music (trumpets lifted from Jeramiah Clarke's 'Prince of Denmark's March') and contemporary pop (the use of a verse from the Merseys' 1966 hit 'Sorrow') anticipated the age of sampling with a far greater vengeance than anything they had previously committed to disc. Add to this Harrison's wonderfully mysterious 'Only a Northern Song' (one can only speculate as to why it was discarded from *Sergeant Pepper*) and one of Lennon's most powerful acid-rock songs to date ('Hey Bulldog'), and one begins to wonder why the album performed less well than its predecessors.

There is, however, another possible reason for the album's comparatively poor performance in the marketplace. Prior to its release, in November and December 1968, the first two solo Beatles projects, Harrison's brilliant *Wonderwall Music* film soundtrack and Lennon and Yoko Ono's avant-garde sound collages, *Unfinished Music No.1 – Two Virgins*, had been released to hostile reviews from the British and American music press and extremely poor sales, the latter record causing furore in some corners because of its provocative cover, which showed Lennon and his new lover/collaborator glaring at the camera in full-frontal nudity.[40] Although agreeing to manufacture the record, EMI refused to distribute it, the job finally being given to the Who's label, Track, who ensured against legal liabilities by packaging the original cover in plain brown wrappers before distributing it. Whilst doubtless appealing to underground factions, neither the cover (which was perceived by many to be pornographic), nor the material it contained impressed the Beatles' mainstream followers, and it is quite possible that the *Yellow Submarine* soundtrack suffered as a result of the hostility generated by these releases. As if this weren't enough, the period between the film and album release was also marked by Lennon's arrest on 18 October 1968 for possession of marijuana. He was released on bail, and in November he was fined £150 at Marylebone Magistrates Court. Although he claimed the incident to have been a set-up, it again fuelled the establishment's disenchantment with the Beatles, who seemed, in the heady months following the film's release, to have destroyed forever their relationship with mainstream followers. As

Lennon himself maintained, 'The trouble is, I suppose, I've spoiled my image. People want me to stay in their own bag. They want me to be loveable. But I was never that. Even at school I was just "Lennon". Nobody ever thought of me as cuddly.'[41]

Despite the LP fiasco, the film spawned a wave of other film-related merchandise in Britain and America with a range of goods which far surpassed the records and novelizations released to coincide with their previous screen incarnations. These products were largely targeted at younger children and, according to Richard Buskin, were launched by over twenty-five licensed merchandisers.[42] As Buskin's book *Beatle Crazy!* illustrates, there was a vast range of children's products, including jigsaws, snowdomes, Halloween costumes, alarm clocks, mobiles, watches and badges.[43] Indeed, on the day of the film's British premiere, the *Evening News* carried an advertisement feature (presumably financed through King Features) titled 'How the Beatles Brought Love Back into Our Funny World', which, as well as advertising the film itself, also contained publicity for Marshall Dee's official *Yellow Submarine* T-shirts (for adults and children) and the New English Library's paperback novelization-cum-picture book, which was proudly proclaimed to be the world's first ever full-colour paperback.[44] Interestingly, the accompanying article claimed that 'John Lennon and Paul McCartney made sizeable contributions to the script of *Yellow Submarine*,'[45] which, while a gross exaggeration, supports Barrow's earlier comments that, upon seeing the finished product, the Beatles were happy not only to publicize the film by attending its premiere, but also to put their creative reputations on the line by lending their names to the project.

Beyond its commercial implications, the critical success of *Yellow Submarine* was of great importance to the group since, for all its drug-induced imagery, it presented the public with the cosy, safe and affable Beatles they knew and loved, deflecting, albeit briefly, the hostility garnered by *Magical Mystery Tour*, the LSD controversy of 1967, and the derision which, in the month of the film's release, had met Lennon and Ono's 'You Are Here' exhibition at the Robert Fraser gallery.[46] As the *Daily Telegraph* nostalgically proclaimed, 'The Beatles spirit is here if not the flesh – their good-natured gusto, their kindly curiosity, their sympathy with their fellow men and their lack of pretentiousness are all summed up here with gaiety.'[47] Although, as I mentioned earlier, this goodwill was somewhat shortlived, *Yellow Submarine* was important to the group's increasingly controversial late sixties image in that it pacified the mainstream press and public by providing a tonic for the group's increasingly bewildering and erratic output and behaviour. 1968 had been the strangest year to date in the Beatles' increasingly diverse career, full of huge peaks and sharp inclines. Though the year began badly with the negative response to *Magical Mystery Tour* still ringing in their ears, they had clawed their way back to mass popularity with the massive-selling 'Hey Jude' and 'Lady Madonna' singles and had reconciled this success with the *Yellow Submarine* movie, only to find the year ending on similar bittersweet notes as the winter of 1967.

Despite the commercial and critical success which heralded the release of their eclectic if rather patchy double album, *The Beatles*, Lennon's arrest and solo activities meant that the year also ended with more artistic, drug-related and (a first for the Beatles) sexual controversy. Worse still, the group's own personal and musical relationships (perhaps compounded by Yoko's constant presence in the recording studio) were beginning to deteriorate beyond repair. During the recording of *The Beatles* LP, Ringo quit the group for two weeks following arguments with the other members. While he was away the group simply went on with the recording sessions, with McCartney effortlessly providing the rhythm tracks for 'Back in the USSR' and 'Dear Prudence'.[48] Following Lennon's inauguration into the experimental styles of Cage and Stockhausen, McCartney desperately tried to keep Lennon and Ono's avant-garde sound collage, 'Revolution 9', off the album, only to meet with Lennon's equally dogged determination for it to remain there. Producer George Martin had recommended that the LP be scaled down to a single but was overruled by the group, and despite the sheer enormity of its eclectic pastiche (hardly a single musical style, contemporary or modern, went unnoticed), the album was essentially the work of four separate musicians working on their own solo numbers. Despite the tally of thirty songs, the recording sessions were frequently conducted in the absence of a complete line-up and, although largely unnoticed at the time, Lennon and McCartney's waning collaborative urge had all but disappeared.

In this sense, *The Beatles* can be seen as something of a watershed album for the group, the first album which contained no collaborative equivalent to 'A Day in the Life' or 'With a Little Help from My Friends', and which highlighted the increasing differences of style of two songwriters who had effectively outgrown the healthy competition which had previously driven them. Whilst Lennon's songs had become increasingly lyrical, personal, and, in the case of 'Revolution 9', avant-garde, McCartney retained and developed his extraordinary melodic skills and uncanny aptitude for musical pastiche. Indeed, while the album's eclecticism and emphasis on the personal and the avant-garde justly won the approval of critics and consumers, there can be little doubt that many of the songs on *The Beatles* lacked the melodic polish they had come to love. Indeed, although the album was a fascinating scrapbook of material (in some ways the group's most 'interesting' piece), many of the numbers lacked the stirring middle-eights and meticulously crafted arrangements so apparent in their more collaborative work, giving credence to George Martin's belief that the record would have been more memorable if scaled down to single-album length.

Worse still, many of the divisions of their recently founded Apple Corps. business were in a mess. Apart from its record division (which, besides the Beatles, had under its supervision such profitable artists as Mary Hopkin), the company's multiplicity of other sections had produced virtually nothing of serious financial worth, and the openhanded ideals to which it aspired were being increasingly exploited from inside and out. On 31 July 1968, just seven months after its opening, the Apple boutique on Baker Street closed down, and its remaining stock was given away to the public. *Magical Mystery Tour* had met with vehement criticism, and Apple Electronics, headed by Lennon's Greek inventor friend 'magic' Alexis Mardas, had failed to produce any viable prototypes, despite the fact that the Beatles had channelled thousands of pounds into providing a working laboratory for the eccentric inventor. Indeed, by the end of the year, Mardas had designed nothing more than an electronic apple which pulsated to light and sound, and a 'nothing box', a construction which, equipped with twelve lights programmed to flash randomly for five years, did – as its name suggested – absolutely nothing of any practical purpose.

The Beatles had initially intended the Apple venture to be a form of 'western communism' in which the 'bosses aren't in it for profit',[49] and on 11 May 1968 Lennon and McCartney had gone to New York to appear on the *Johnny Carson Show*, where they announced their plans to patronize artists from all cultural disciplines. As McCartney had maintained at an American press conference, 'If you come to me and say, "I've had such and such a dream," I will say, "Here's so much money. Go away and do it." We've already bought all our dreams, so now we want to share that possibility with others.'[50] Two weeks earlier, full-page advertisements had appeared in the British music press, urging would-be recording artists to send in tapes to the Apple Music offices, and within days the London offices were flooded by a tidal wave of tapes, poems, film scripts and novels. At one point Denis O'Dell had five full-time readers wading through piles of unsolicited film scripts,[51] and, despite the best efforts of managing director Neil Aspinall and press officer Derek Taylor it was impossible to deal with the endless onslaught of applications for funding. As Taylor remembers, 'We tried to do what we promised, to help people realize their dreams, but it was impossible. There weren't sufficient hours in the day or sufficient resources.'[52] The Beatles, for all their extraordinary mastery of musical genres, were not businessmen, and it showed. The Apple was beginning to rot.

Notes

1. Harry, 1984, p. 164. According to Harry, the cartoons were shown only on Granada television.
2. Percentage from Barrow, 1993b, p. 10.
3. McCabe and Schonfeld, 1972, p. 92.
4. Harry, 1984, p. 37.
5. Canemaker, 1986/7, p. 27. According to the author, $200,000 of this figure went to the Beatles 'for the use of their songs'.
6. Lewisohn, 1992, p. 276.
7. Paul Angelis, 'The Real McCartney – Eddie Yates', *Observer*, 4 September 1988.
8. Ibid.
9. Denis O'Dell, interviewed by author, 30 April 1996.
10. Ibid.
11. Martin, 1979, p. 226.
12. Barrow, 1993b, p. 13.
13. Evans, 1984, p. 84.
14. Joel W. Finler, *IT*, 26 July 1968.
15. Avedon produced a set of psychedelic Beatles posters in 1968. According to Evans, 1984, p. 76, they were marketed in Britain through a special offer in the *Daily Express*.
16. Melly, 1970, p. 115.
17. Ibid., p. 137.
18. This eclectic mixture of styles is discussed by Sharman, 1994, pp. 14–15.
19. Miles, 1978, pp. 83–4.
20. Ibid., p. 89.
21. For a fascinating discussion of the Beatles' (and especially Lennon's) relationship to these developments, see MacDonald, 1994, pp. 225–8.
22. Ibid. According to the author, the

song's lyric brought the group considerable controversy with radical bodies such as the controversy with New Left groups, many of whom regarded the pacifistic lyrics as a 'betrayal'.

23. *Variety* review, 23 July 1968.
24. Lewisohn, 1989, p. 164.
25. Trudi Pacter, *Daily Mail*, 29 December 1967.
26. Cecil Wilson, *Daily Mail*, 17 July 1968. Referring to the character of Jeremy, Wilson states: 'He exerts so much charm with his blue face, green eyelids, purple ears and prissy voice that you wonder why Disney never invented him.'
27. Patrick Gibb, *Daily Telegraph*, 19 July 1968; John Russell Taylor, *The Times*, 18 July 1968.
28. 'Lessons at the Movies', Nigel Gosling, *Observer*, 28 July 1968.
29. Gavin Millar, *Sight and Sound*, vol. 37, no. 4, p. 204.
30. Joel W. Finler, *IT*, 26 July 1968.
31. *Esquire*, December 1968.
32. Felix Barker, 'Beatles, Meanies and Stark Raving Bonkers', *Evening News*, 18 July 1968.
33. Judith Simons, *Daily Express*, 6 August 1968.
34. Harry, 1984, p. 46.
35. Brown and Gaines, 1984, p. 191.
36. Harry, 1984, p. 46.
37. Lewisohn, 1989, p. 164.
38. Ibid.
39. Ibid.
40. The Harrison LP, the soundtrack for a pychedelic art movie directed by Joe Massot, was the first record to be released on the Apple label. The vehement critical response to the cover of the Lennon/Ono collaboration was not helped by the hostile and frequently racist press reaction to Lennon and Ono's relationship. Although Lennon and the Japanese concept artist had been lovers since early 1968, Lennon was still married to his first wife, Cynthia, and Ono was labelled as the monster responsible for destroying Lennon's happy marriage.
41. Connolly, 1981, p. 109.
42. Buskin, 1994, p. 84.
43. Ibid.
44. *Evening News*, 17 July 1968.
45. Ibid.
46. This exhibition was essentially a collection of conceptual art produced by Lennon, in collaboration with Yoko Ono. For more information, see Evans, 1984, pp. 92–4.
47. 'Beatles Find Their Film Feet in Weird and Witty Fantasy', *Daily Telegraph*, 17 July 1968.
48. This is not to say that the other Beatles did not miss Starr. When he returned to the studios, he found his drums garlanded with flowers.
49. Giuliano and Giuliano, 1995, p. 87.
50. Ibid.
51. Denis O'Dell, interviewed by author. According to O'Dell, most of these scripts were unreadable.
52. Lawrence Donegan, 'Another Bite at the Apple', *Guardian*, 21 November 1995.

5

TroubledTimes:
Let It Be

Apart from *Magical Mystery Tour*, the Beatles' final film, *Let It Be* (or *Get Back* as it was first called) is undoubtedly the most neglected movie in their canon. Although revered by hardcore fans, the film received scant critical attention in its day and has since been largely ignored by film critics and historians. The reasons for its relative obscurity in film history are not difficult to fathom. The film was not released until months after it was shot, and this, compounded by poor reviews and Lennon's derogatory comments about the recording of the film's music ('It was the most miserable session on earth'[1]), has done little for its reputation. Critical reassessment has been hampered by its subsequent lack of exposure: the British Film Institute does not hold a copy, the film has not been shown on network TV for over a decade, and even now it is the only Beatles movie to have bypassed an official video release. Yet while few would claim *Let It Be* as the Beatles' finest moment, if one cares to scratch its rusty surface, it becomes evident that the movie offers considerable interest to film historian and Beatles scholar alike.

The historical development of the *Let It Be* movie is nothing if not unconventional, not least because it evolved from far humbler origins, as a short television documentary film initially intended to detail the Beatles' rehearsals for a separate and more elaborate television special which never came into fruition. To understand the genesis of the film, one has to return to 1968 and the awkward and disagreeable atmosphere which pervaded the recording sessions for *The Beatles*. The lack of collaboration and increasing reliance on studio technology (and quite possibly evolving personal differences) had convinced McCartney (by now the prime mover in the Beatles' projects) that the flagging group needed to unite and energize itself by returning to their rock and roll roots, producing songs which, bereft of the studio trickery of old, could be performed live. With this in mind, McCartney proposed that the Beatles should work towards putting together a live performance of new material; not a live tour (none of the group could face returning to the rigours of the stadium circuit), but a recorded 'one-off' live performance of new songs which could then be broadcast worldwide as a television special and released as an album. The underlying concept of making a film of a live performance was not new to the Beatles, who had already invested in a concert film for television, *The Beatles at Shea Stadium* (1965). Although not accompanied by an album, this 48-minute document of the group's most celebrated, record-breaking American concert (a co-production between Subafilms, NEMS and Ed Sullivan productions) had attracted huge interest when shown in Britain in 1966 and in America almost a year later. But where would this new live performance take place? In the spirit of underground 'happenings', suggestions were made for suitably 'far-out' locations, but no single venue could be decided by the increasingly individually minded Beatles. One of the first suggestions, which originated from Apple Films' chief Denis O'Dell, was that the group should play at a disused flour mill near the Thames, but this idea was eventually rejected. Another of O'Dell's ideas was for the group to play on board an ocean liner, but this was vetoed for practical reasons. By far the most interesting idea was that the group should play in a Roman amphitheatre in North Africa. As chance would have it, O'Dell had seen an Italian opera company performing *Orestes* in Tripoli, and came up with the fascinating idea of getting the Beatles to perform a live set in front of an Arab audience. As O'Dell recalls, 'It was a wonderful, open-air amphitheatre, right by the sea, with the most incredible acoustic sound ... John flipped. He thought it would be incredible ... but you could never get all four of them to agree.'[2]

Getting agreement on film projects was something that had been difficult with the Beatles for some time. As O'Dell remembers, 'What I wanted to do dearly, and more than anything else, was a major feature film with the Beatles.'[3] In 1968, O'Dell had hit upon a fascinating idea for a third Beatles feature film, that they should make a filmed version of the Tolkein classic, *Lord of the Rings*, for which he attempted to secure the rights and the services of a major director. One possibility was David Lean, who found the idea fascinating but was unavailable.[4] He also approached Stanley Kubrick. According to O'Dell, Kubrick had never read the work. As he remembers it, 'I sent the books round to be read by him. He read them, and his daughter berated him for not ever having read them.'[5] Meanwhile he managed to get the Beatles interested whilst on their trip to visit the Maharishi in Rishikesh, India. 'John was really excited about doing the music for it,'[6] and the group began to earmark parts for themselves. However, having read the books and met with both Lennon and McCartney over lunch at MGM studios, Kubrick maintained that he felt the film was unmakeable, and eventually the project fell through.[7]

When, in late 1968, it was finally agreed to begin rehearsals for the live performance television special (to be shot at an unspecified location), O'Dell suggested that the preparations should be filmed for a separate half-hour television documentary showing the Beatles at work. 'I thought it would be an awful waste not to put everything on film.'[8] With this in mind, it was decided that Twickenham film studios would provide an ideal location for the rehearsals and Michael Lindsay-Hogg (who had worked on several Beatles promos) was hired, to document the sessions by impassively capturing the Beatles 'au naturel'. There were to be few concessions to classical documentary techniques, the idea being that merely showing the Beatles rehearsing and interacting would hold the audience's interest and provide insight into the group's relationships and activities. Lindsay-Hogg explained later: 'I didn't want to make a straight documentary. I figured if we just showed them working, we'd learn quite a bit about them.'[9] In keeping with this premise, 'staged' visual concessions would be kept to a minimum (a few coloured lights to provide ambience) and the rehearsals would be shot in their totality, complete with the talking, rapping and humorous banter which went on between songs. This approach, whilst in keeping with the rawness and honesty of the musical material, was also partly reflective of certain other trends in the pop documentary. While the desire to document the creative process had been exploited by their friends the Rolling Stones in Godard's *One Plus One: Sympathy for the Devil* (1968), the film was perhaps also partly inspired by the direct cinema of independent American documentarists such as Richard Leacock and D. A. Pennebaker, whose *Don't Look Back* (1966) and *Monterey Pop* (1968) had fundamentally focused upon impassively capturing the intimate 'backstage' moments of public personalities.

Filming (on 16mm), began at Twickenham studios, on the first day of rehearsals 2 January 1969. However, the sessions got off to a terrible start, with the Beatles struggling desperately to find a new musical direction. As the filmtrack bootlegs testify, the group spent most of the first week in a largely directionless flux and, although some of the work was productive, the majority of the sessions were characterized by tired reworkings of old, discarded originals ('One After 909'), perfunctory covers of their old rock and roll favourites ('Hi Heel Sneakers', 'Memphis Tennessee') and uninspired jamming. Even when a member of the group brought in some new material, the Beatles seemed unable to approach it as a cohesive unit, and when Harrison, Starr and McCartney tackled the aptly titled 'I Me Mine', the apathetic and preoccupied Lennon was more interested in waltzing around the studios with the ever-present Yoko than contributing his musical presence.

In retrospect, it is not surprising that the sessions got off to such a poor start. The Beatles had long since abandoned their live performances in favour of the studio, and they were inevitably going to be rusty when it came to ensemble work. Moreover, the strain of endlessly producing new material had to catch up with them eventually; the accomplished but sprawling *White Album* had eaten up twenty-five of Lennon and McCartney's most recent compositions, and now, just eleven weeks after those sessions were complete, they found themselves struggling to match up to the tough goal they had set themselves. This problem was compounded by the fact that neither the filming schedule nor the oppressive atmosphere of Twickenham were conducive to the spirit of improvisation that the situation demanded. The early morning starts were deeply oppressive for a band that for years had worked mainly at nights, and the cold enormity of the Twickenham sound stage was a far cry from the relative intimacy of Abbey Road.

After a week of bickering, boredom and apathy, George Harrison snapped. Following an argument with McCartney he quit the stage and, with a non-committal parting shot of 'See you round the clubs',[10] he returned to his bungalow in Esher. As Harrison recently recalled, 'I thought I'm quite capable of being relatively happy on my own and I'm not able to be happy in this situation... I'm getting out of here.'[11] The Beatles were fragmenting at an alarming rate.

Harrison's disappearance inevitably created something of a dilemma for the film-makers. However, Denis O'Dell wisely recognized the importance of 'keeping the remains of [the project] together',[12] and instructed Lindsay-Hogg to spend the next few days on close-shots of

McCartney, Lennon and Starr which could later be edited into the film. Accordingly, in the days following Harrison's departure, the remaining members of the group returned to Twickenham and went about their business in much the same fashion as when Starr had 'left' during the *White Album* sessions, with the cameras still rolling. But when, on 15 January, Harrison returned to the fold, he did so on condition that the live concert should be axed and that the Beatles should instead make an album of the songs which they had been working on in the newly built recording studio at their Apple headquarters. Mark Lewisohn claims: 'It was at this point, and this point only, that the footage shot at Twickenham for a 'Beatles at Work' television production turned instead into the start of a feature film idea, to be called – like the album they'd now be making – *Get Back*'.[13] Useful though these insights are, they do not explain the reasoning behind the idea to elevate the status of the initially low-key, by-product project by turning it into a full-length documentary feature film (for television, or possibly theatrical exhibition) which was now intended to chart the group's progression from rough rehearsal to polished recording rather than live performance. However, there are a number of possible artistic and economic factors which can be identified to account for the switch.

The Beatles may have felt that, since the idea for the live concert had been jettisoned, they should instead appease their audience with something more substantial than a thirty-minute television documentary. There was certainly no particular reason for *not* making the film. After all, because of its minimalist aesthetic, the film's production would require little, if any, additional commitment from the fragmenting group. All they had to do was turn up at the Apple studios where the cameras would capture them doing what they did best – producing albums. Moreover, since there was no essential difference between rehearsing new songs for an album or for a live concert, the footage shot at Twickenham could and would still be included. Not only that, producing the film through Apple (Denis O'Dell and Neil Aspinall would helm the production and the Beatles would retain the role of executive producers[14]) meant that they had ultimate control of the film's style and content. Moreover, they still owed, or possibly felt they owed, United Artists a final film. *Yellow Submarine* had been rejected by UA on the grounds that their contract required films starring the group rather than cartoon representations of them; and since, by

1969, it appeared increasingly evident that the group would be either unprepared or unable to agree upon a project in which they would have to act, elevating the status of the short television documentary into something more substantial was a possible way of satisfying all parties. However, although they later accepted the film and blew it up for theatrical release, no negotiations took place between Apple and UA during the film shooting, suggesting that appeasing the US major was not, at this point in the proceedings, part of the equation.[15]

Although the group had given in to Harrison's demand to abandon live performance, there was a kind of compromise; the album would still be recorded with a quasi-'live' aesthetic and the new Beatles album and film would employ, as the working title implied, a 'back to basics' approach. There would be none of the high-tech studio trickery so prevalent since *Revolver*, the recordings would not be overdubbed at all, any mistakes would remain intact, and the emphasis would be on resummoning the rock and roll spirit of their formative years. As Philip Norman so succinctly put it, 'It was as if, to rediscover themselves as musicians, they were putting themselves through the kind of endurance test that Hamburg used to be; seeking to re-activate those old, tight sinews with music that stretched back to their collective birth.'[16] However, relationships were still strained. Working on the principle that people behave better in company, Harrison drafted in another musician, the soul singer and pianist Billy Preston, to help relieve the tension and provide inspiration for the tired Beatles. According to Harrison, when Preston was brought in there was a 'one hundred per cent improvement'[17] in the strained atmosphere.

However, despite the seductiveness of its alluring premise, and Harrison's subtle attempt to temper the hostilities, both shooting and recording were initially hampered by practical problems. The Beatles had planned to restart the project on Monday 20 January in the basement studio newly constructed for the group by the Greek electronics 'expert', 'magic' Alexis Mardas of Apple's electronic division. Having impressed Lennon with a number of his ideas and prototypes for various products, Mardas had convinced the Beatles that the recording equipment at Abbey Road was antiquated and that he could construct a state-of-the-art studio which would far outclass the technology of Abbey Road by providing seventy-two track recording. Although the studio was due to be ready for the group's use on this day, it became patently apparent upon their arrival that Mardas' bizarre designs were unable to live up to their inventor's claims, and filming and recording were delayed by two days while the ever reliable George Martin negotiated the use of mobile recording equipment from Abbey Road. When the necessary technology did arrive, the sessions were infinitely more enjoyable and productive than they had been at Twickenham and, while it would be inaccurate to suggest that they were totally successful in harnessing the group's true live potential, the group refined and recorded a number of new and inspired songs (including Harrison's 'For You Blue' and McCartney's wonderful 'Get Back'). However, progress was still somewhat slow, and sessions would often take a similar manifestation as they had at Twickenham, with productivity giving way to impromptu jamming and mainly insipid covers.

This was of little help to Lindsay-Hogg. Despite having shot hours of fascinating, if sombre footage of the Beatles jamming and recording (interspersed with all the extra-musical footage of the group clowning around, arguing, telling jokes, and soberly discussing their future plans between songs), the director's material still lacked an adequate resolution or suitably professional musical 'climax'. Indeed, despite having shot a total of three weeks' rehearsal/recording footage, the film still lacked enough suitably polished or completed performances and, since Beatles albums had been known to take months to complete, the idea of merely continuing in the same vein seemed both impractical and inadequate for all parties.

Out of this frustration, on 26 January came the suggestion that the group should play an impromptu live performance on the rooftop of Apple's Savile Row headquarters, to be filmed by Lindsay-Hogg as the climax of the movie. Harrison was apparently still hesitant about the idea but eventually gave in to pressure from the others, and on 30 January 1969 the Beatles played spirited versions of *Get Back*, 'I've Got a Feeling', 'Dig a Pony', 'Don't Let Me Down' and 'One After 909' to the cameras and the bewildered crowd of office workers who were milling around Savile Row in their lunch hour. The concert 'happening' was a triumph. After three weeks of apathy, indecision and slow progress, the Beatles had finally managed to rekindle their ability to generate the excitement of their spellbinding live performances, and once again they proved that when they put their personal and artistic differences behind them, they were consummate ensemble players. Along with their musical rebirth came the return of their acerbic wit. As the police finally made it through the Apple offices and onto the roof to break up the noisy party, Lennon, perhaps sensing that the concert would be their final live performance, ironically remarked, 'I'd like to say thank you on behalf of the group and ourselves, and I hope we passed the audition!'

However, the rooftop performance was not, as has been frequently documented, the end of the *Get Back* shoot. Perhaps realizing that they still needed more polished numbers for a commercial film release (be it for television or cinema), they completed shooting the following day at the Apple basement studio, with note-perfect live performances of the finished versions of 'Let It Be', 'The Long and Winding Road' and 'Two of Us'.

Although shooting for the film was completed in January 1969, it would be May 1970 before it was released, largely because of delays in the preparation of the accompanying album. With the recording sessions complete, neither George Martin nor the Beatles could bring themselves to begin painfully trawling through the hours of tapes and attempting to edit and mix them into a listenable soundtrack album. Although two songs from the *Get Back* recording sessions were released in single form soon after their recording ('Get Back' and 'Don't Let Me Down' were issued as a highly successful single in April 1969 complete with promotional clips culled from the film), the Beatles' flagging interest was compounded by two other important factors.

Firstly, by the end of April 1969 the Beatles were already busy recording what was to become their final collaboration, the *Abbey Road* album. Secondly, by mid to late 1969 and the completion of *Abbey Road*, they were even closer to what would become their final split. Although it is not for this book to discuss the non-filmic aspects of the group's affairs in detail, it is worth noting that Apple was by now in a state of financial and administrative turmoil, there were severe disagreements over the employment of Allen Klein as manager, and the Beatles' artistic differences were becoming even more pronounced. Lennon had become obsessed with collaborating artistically with Yoko Ono, with whom he produced another collection of sound collages *(Unfinished Music 2: Life with the Lions)*, and a series of short avant-garde films such as *Smile* (1968), *Apotheosis* (1969) and *Legs* (1970).

He married her in March 1969. McCartney had also become interested in solo projects, as had Harrison, who, possibly frustrated by his small song allowance on Beatles albums, was fast emerging from the shadow of Lennon and McCartney as a major songwriter in his own right. His contributions to the Beatles' *Abbey Road*, 'Here Comes the Sun' and 'Something', were arguably the most memorable tracks on the album, the latter song gaining a single release, becoming an evergreen standard and being described by Frank Sinatra as 'the greatest love song of the past fifty years'.[18] Starr, meanwhile, was keen to develop his acting talents. In September 1969, Lennon privately told the others that he wanted 'a divorce',[19] and, although it would be 10 April 1970 before McCartney publicly announced that the Beatles were effectively over, the group were practically finished as a functioning, creative unit at this point, with harmonious musical collaboration all but dissolving into complex business disagreements and bitter feuds. Indeed, it has been alleged in several places that the reason the break was not announced in September was because Klein was in the process of sensitive renegotiations of the Beatles' recording contract with EMI and did not want to upset the applecart.[20]

However, although the fragmenting Beatles were busy with other projects and distractions in the months following the sessions, work on the album did not completely stop. In March 1969, the group's then engineer, Glyn Johns, had been given the difficult task of mixing the album, but Lennon, Harrison and Allen Klein were reportedly unhappy with the mix and in early 1970, shortly after the release of the *Abbey Road* album, they commissioned American producer Phil Spector to perform a salvage job on the tapes. Spector carried out his task by adding treacly strings and melodramatic heavenly choirs to the original recordings, undermining the entire *raison d'être* of the 'live' aesthetic and increasing (if it was possible) the bitter artistic rifts between the group. While Lennon later praised Spector's work and maintained that he 'was given the shittiest load of badly recorded shit with a lousy feeling to it ever, and he made something out of it',[21] McCartney was particularly annoyed to hear his haunting 'Long and Winding Road' ballad stripped of its stark simplicity and dressed up in an ocean of clichéd sentimental strings.

Eventually, however, Spector's version of the album was released, along with the film (minus Spector's polish), in May 1970, sixteen months after work had begun on the project and just weeks after news of the group's demise. The film, now significantly retitled *Let It Be*, received a world premiere in New York on 13 May. Unsurprisingly, none of the Beatles attended.

With the exception of the final day's studio footage, which is neatly edited into the middle section, the final cut of the film sticks fairly faithfully to the initial plan of chronicling the Beatles' progression from rough rehearsal to polished studio performances, with the rooftop concert providing additional excitement as the film's musical climax. With the footage divided into more or less temporally balanced sections of approximately twenty-five to thirty minutes, the movie is effectively structured into a triptych of chronological 'acts' (Twickenham, the Apple studio, the rooftop), their conclusions emphasized by pronounced wipes.

Although conventionally chronological, the film's form is not without interest, not least because it is one of the most minimalist films to attain a full theatrical release in Britain. As well as avoiding the classical documentary techniques of reportage and interview, the edited film lacks the traditional narrative signifiers of temporal construction, and although the audience must naturally assume that the acts of the triptych are presented chronologically, there are no titles or voice-over narration to clarify this. Indeed, beyond the 'correct' ordering of the sequences, the only other sense of temporal progression is provided by the increasingly accomplished musicianship of the Beatles, and in this sense *Let It Be* really does 'let the music do the talking'. In a similar manner, the film also avoids conventional signifiers of place, and with the exception of a few grainy shots of the Beatles entering the Apple offices, the audience is provided with very little information about where the group are playing. By avoiding these conventions, the film focuses the viewer's attentions entirely upon the Beatles' performances/relationships, and imbues them with a mythical sense of timelessness and universality. Indeed, as Jonathan Cott and David Dalton maintain, 'If *A Hard Day's Night* portrayed the Beatles' "real life" image as fiction, and if *Yellow Submarine* embodied that image mythically, *Let It Be* documents a few moments of the Beatles together "awake" and "for real".'[22]

Such minimalist techniques possibly grew from a number of influences. Whilst the idea of avoiding conventional signifiers is probably derived from the counter-culture's distrust of traditional form, it also seems highly derivative of American direct cinema. Indeed, if the initial 'invisible camera' approach and 'backstage' aesthetic of the project was derivative of much of Pennebaker's work, then so too were the film's editing techniques, which in their anti-institutional refusal to employ such conventional signifiers also place emphasis upon capturing the 'essence' rather than the historicity of events. Although made under vastly different circumstances from Pennebaker's masterpiece *Don't Look Back* (as well as having far more elaborate production values, the rooftop sequence was clearly staged specifically for the film), *Let It Be* is similar in spirit (if not content), and the similarities certainly add credence to the idea posited in Chapter Three, that the Beatles admired Dylan's 'truthful' presentation in *Don't Look Back* and wanted to make a similar film of themselves. Indeed, if *Magical Mystery Tour* can be said to absorb some of the Dylan film's characteristics, then *Let It Be* bought into direct cinema with greater tenacity.

Beyond its form, *Let It Be* is, at least for admirers of the Beatles, of great interest. The rawness of the film's colossal soundtrack (around twenty songs) documents the manner in which the group, in their return to rock and roll, had gone full circle musically (something emphasized by the original discarded cover for the accompanying album, which featured a modern recreation of the *Please Please Me* LP photographs), and by employing a 'fly-on-the-wall' approach Lindsay-Hogg allows audiences the fascinating opportunity to eavesdrop upon the Beatles' rehearsals and recordings with a voyeurism which is a fascinating, if at times painful, experience. Whatever one's opinion of *Let It Be*, it is impossible to deny the film's honesty. It makes no secret of the fact that the Beatles are in the process of splitting up and, although any sequences filmed in Harrison's absence are edited out, there are scenes which pull no punches in laying bear the stark reality that the group are no longer working in a state of artistic harmony. This is particularly evident towards the end of the Twickenham footage, where we see McCartney (who was clearly the dominant artistic and motivating force behind the Beatles in the *Let It Be* sessions) patronizing Harrison about his musicianship and Harrison retorting that 'I'll play whatever you want me to play or I won't play at all if you don't want me to play. Whatever it is that will please you – I'll do it.' It is a deeply unsettling sequence, and one finds oneself squirming with a sense of guilty embarrassment as the Beatles expose the open wounds of their relationships for public consumption.

Although the film was obviously envisaged as a 'real' document, it is nevertheless surprising that the Beatles should let such painful footage pass into the film. That they did is the result of one or two different possibilities. Either by this point they simply didn't care about how they were represented since they were splitting up anyway or, and this, I think, is the most likely explanation, there was a part of them which actively wanted to show the world that they were at the end of their personal and artistic tethers. After all, when Glyn Johns had mixed the original album without overdubs, the group had been tempted to release them in their roughest possible form, Lennon commenting in retrospect that 'I thought it would be good to go out, the shitty version, because it would break the Beatles, you know, it would break the myth. That's us, with no trousers on and no glossy paint over the cover and no sort of hope. This is what we are like with our trousers off, so would you please end the game now.'[23] Although, as we have seen, this did not happen and the soundtrack for the album was 'salvaged' by Spector, the group were probably unprepared to make similar commercial compromises for the film, which, with its unaltered soundtrack and frequently unflattering depiction of themselves, they perhaps believed would demolish their myth once and for all. If this is true, then they were sadly mistaken on both counts. While the argument footage makes fascinating, if harrowing, viewing, the unadulterated film soundtrack is, in spite (indeed, because of) its rawness and at times inspired urgency, infinitely more rewarding than the cheap kitsch and gratuitous sentimentality of Spector's superimpositions, and for all Lennon's subsequent praise of the producer's remake there is, at least for most fans, no comparison between the two versions. One can only hope that the original mix of the shelved *Get Back* album will materialize in its entirety at some point in the future.

Despite its endearing honesty, however, it must be conceded that the film is flawed. Most importantly, it fails, at least partially, to provide the audience with the single element one imagines it wants most: a detailed understanding of the creative evolution behind the Beatles' songs. Despite witnessing the progression of the group's musical prowess, the audience are largely denied the opportunity of experiencing the creative evolution of individual songs and, with a few minor exceptions (most notably, 'Don't Let Me Down' and 'The Long and Winding Road'), the film concentrates instead upon presenting as many different numbers as possible. We see nothing of how the film's most polished lynchpin songs are developed, with numbers such as 'Let It Be' and 'Get Back' presented only in their finished versions. This, to my mind, is a great shame and ultimately something of a mistake. While the evolution of the film's title track is not of special interest, the development of McCartney's 'Get Back' went through a fascinating and lengthy series of changes. Originally a satire on contemporary British immigration issues (titled 'Commonwealth Song' and 'Don't Dig No Pakistanis' on bootleg albums), it is to the film's detriment that its gradual blossoming is absent from the final print. Moreover, despite the fact that the film attempts to cram as many numbers as possible into its discourse, its judgement over what to include and what to exclude frequently seems shaky at best. While McCartney's charming 'Teddy Boy' (originally included in the Glyn Johns mix of the *Get Back* album and later reworked for McCartney's own self-titled debut release) fails to make an appearance in the film, so too does Harrison's transcendental 'All Things Must Pass', which he later recorded as the title track of his massive-selling post-Beatles debut in 1970. The exclusion of the latter song is particularly surprising. While arguably the most poetic and harmonious song Harrison had produced thus far, it was also a neat, if abstract, philosophical description of the group's current situation, and far superior to either of his other contributions towards the finished film's soundtrack.

Another central flaw is that the film provides less insight into the group's personal relationships than its publicity boasted (trailers maintained that the film would show the group 'rapping', 'relaxing' and 'philosophizing'). Although, amongst the songs, the final cut presents the audience with moments which are by turns amusing, enthralling and harrowing (Lennon's rendition of the 'Queen Says No to Pot-Smoking FBI Members' newspaper headline, McCartney and Starr's charming piano boogie duet, McCartney attempting to persuade an uninterested Lennon that the group should make another film), these are few and far between and there is little real dialogue and/or non-musical interaction. Indeed, beyond learning that the Beatles are experiencing musical differences and that Paul McCartney is the most enthusiastic member of the group, one is left with little idea about the Beatles' 'philosophies', musical or otherwise. As Nina Hibbin of the *Morning Star* was later to comment, 'For those expecting it to throw some light on the development of the Beatles phenomenon, it is disappointingly barren.'[24]

Reviews were almost unanimously scathing. The album package, which consisted of an elaborate box housing the record, a souvenir book of film stills and dialogue from the sessions (produced through Apple's publishing division), was heavily criticized by reviewers for its short weight of twelve songs and the high price which the inclusion of the book necessitated. Indeed, the album was generally regarded as 'a cheapskate epitaph'[25] by the majority of critics, and the film fared little better. Although publications with youthful and/or underground sympathies predictably praised the documentary's form and candour, the mainstream British press, despite some praise for the soundtrack music, bombarded the film with criticisms. While some of these were justified (and there can be little doubt that the film *is* unsatisfactory in some respects), many contemporary reviews seem in retrospect to betray a hostility which, no doubt born of the sentimental, conservative notion that the Beatles should be making elaborate, 'feelgood' comedies and not 'serious' documentaries (and especially not minimalist, sombre, and theatrically released ones), display a blind refusal to accept or even to consider the film on its own generic terms. To criticize the film's sparsity of insight is one thing, but to lampoon, as did the *Daily Sketch*, a cine-direct documentary for its less than crystal-clear sound and picture quality,[26] or the Beatles, for being 'dull and unfunny' (as did the *Evening Standard*[27]), is rather like a horror buff pouring scorn on a romantic drama for it not being sufficiently terrifying. In this sense many of the press complaints mirror the earlier banalities that *Magical Mystery Tour* had 'no story'.

Yet while the 'documentary' Beatles of 1970 were as unpopular with the critics as the 'avant-garde' ones had been some three years earlier, the legions of fans were not so easily deterred. Although it was less successful than the Lester films, both *Let It Be* and accompanying soundtrack album attained respectable posthumous commercial success in both Britain and America. Moreover, the Beatles were awarded an Oscar for best score.

To the best of my knowledge, there are no plans to rerelease the film commercially, and most British fans will have to be content with the thousands of scratchy bootlegs which have been circulating around record fairs since the advent of video. Yet for those fans lucky enough to see it, the 'real-life' authenticity of *Let It Be* continues to exalt a musical spontaneity and voyeuristic pleasure which is by nature absent from the other movies. According to Jonathan Cott and David Dalton, 'It is one of the paradoxes of reverence that we always wish to know the most intimate details of those we idolize, even when the details are not flattering ...'[28] I have mixed feelings about the film in this sense. As both fan and film enthusiast, it is, for me, both the 'worst' and the 'best' Beatles movie, unsatisfactory (although interesting) as a piece of film-making, and fascinating for both its musical and non-musical content.

That said, it is not unreasonable to suggest that time has been kinder to *Let It Be* than it actually deserves. One suspects that, shorn of its historical significance, it would exert much less interest and mystique than it now does (should I say, could?) and in this sense it is interesting to make an analogy between the film and Van Gogh's final painting, *Cornfield with Crows*. In his fascinating book *Ways of Seeing*, John Berger brilliantly demonstrates how the 'baggage' of historical context determines the retrospective perception of cultural artefacts,[29] and *Let It Be*, like Van Gogh's final painting, carries plenty of 'baggage'. If the Beatles hadn't split, and if Van Gogh hadn't killed himself, their final works would perhaps attract lesser interest from their devotees, although the degree of this 'lesser interest' is ultimately and inevitably unquantifiable. But the Beatles did split, and that split sent tremors throughout the global cultural landscape. As Mark Hertsgaard points out, their split took on 'a far larger historical significance than the demise of mere pop stars; rather, like the assassination of presidents or the July 1969 moon landing, the breakup of the Beatles was regarded as one of the defining events of the sixties. Indeed, seizing on the fact that the split came a scant four months into the new decade, media pundits invariably interpreted it as a sign that the sixties era of optimism and goodwill had conclusively ended.'[30]

In the final anaysis, it is this 'historical significance' upon which, rightly or wrongly, the reputation of the film will probably be ultimately judged. Whatever criticisms can be levelled at the film, it must be acknowledged that its timing, like virtually everything else in the Beatles' canon, was alchemic. As the reviewer for *Time* magazine so succinctly put it, *Let It Be* is 'instant history'.[31]

Notes

1. Miles, 1978, p. 113.
2. Denis O'Dell, interviewed by author, 30 April 1996.
3. Ibid.
4. Ibid. O'Dell felt that Lean would have been 'marvellous for the Beatles'. O'Dell perhaps rightly believed that, apart from his directorial skills, Lean's seniority would enable him to assume a 'father figure' role which would afford him the respect necessary to work productively with the group.
5. Ibid.
6. Ibid.
7. Ibid. According to O'Dell, it transpired that United Artists already owned the film rights to *Lord of the Rings* and were prepared to allow the script to be made into a third Beatles film if the services of a major director could be secured. This never happened, and subsequent attempts to transfer the film rights to Apple proved unsuccessful.
8. Ibid.
9. Jerry Hopkins, 'The Trouble with the Beatles', *Rolling Stone*, 9 July 1970, p. 12.
10. Lewisohn, 1992, p. 307.
11. *The Beatles Anthology* (Apple, 1995).
12. Denis O'Dell, interviewed by author.
13. Lewisohn, 1992, p. 307.
14. Denis O'Dell, interviewed by author. O'Dell is not credited on the film titles despite having been largely responsible for setting up the production, which Aspinall then took over as O'Dell became more and more involved in setting up *The Magic Christian*, shot shortly after *Let It Be*. According to O'Dell, 'I gave it [the credit] to Neil because he wanted to be a producer' and because 'in the final analysis he did more work on it than I did'.
15. Ibid. Furthermore, O'Dell believes that United Artists' option on a third movie had, by this point in the Beatles' career, expired under English law, the basis upon which the original three-film contract had been agreed.
16. Norman, 1981, p. 358.
17. *The Beatles Anthology* (Apple, 1995).
18. MacDonald, 1994, p. 278.
19. Lewisohn, 1992, p. 340.
20. See for example, Hertsgaard, 1995, p. 280.
21. Wenner, 1973, p. 120.
22. Cott and Dalton, 1970, p. 21.
23. Wenner, 1973, p. 120–2.
24. Nina Hibbin, *Morning Star*, 23 May 1970.
25. Lewisohn, 1992, p. 340.
26. 'A Washout and It Even Sounds Poor', Robert Ottoway, *Daily Sketch*, 20 May 1970. Ottoway describes the project as a 'low-fi LP-on-film'.
27. Alexander Walker, *Evening Standard*, 2 May 1970.
28. Cott and Dalton, 1970, p. 22.
29. Berger, 1972, pp. 27–8.
30. Hertsgaard, 1995, pp. 277–8.
31. Review, *Time*, 8 June 1970.

6

Revolution:
The Impact of the Beatles Movies

Although the Beatles' film history ends with *Let It Be*, the group's films, like their music, continue to exert significant impact and influence. The movies have received less critical coverage than the music, but in many ways they were as innovatory as the soundtrack material which accompanied them. Discussing both their collective impact and commercial popularity is, however, as potentially problematic as assessing their musical output in such a manner, not least because of the formal, ideological and economic differences between each film.

Indeed, although we have traced certain links between the films in the preceding chapters, the overwhelming impression which they collectively exude is one of stylistic dissimilarity and experimentation. Yet it is this stylistic diversity and tendency towards the experimental and the avant-garde which paradoxically links the films rather neatly together. From Lester's rejection of the performance aesthetic to *Magical Mystery Tour's* refusal of narrative logic, and from *Yellow Submarine's* untried cartoon pop musical feature format to *Let It Be's* minimalism, a spirit of experimentation permeates the films from beginning to end, putting paid to the popular film-historical assumption that all movies funded and/or distributed by American companies are carefully controlled by their backers and ruthlessly moulded to conform exactly to the dominant narrative patterns and formulaic precedents of what has long been regarded by reductive film histories as an intrinsically 'American' film style.

That each Beatles film was so stylistically different from its own predecessors and from the classical pop musical in general is perhaps a tribute to both their makers' creativity and, from a broader perspective, to the Beatles' unrelenting desire to immerse themselves and their collaborators in experimentation. Unlike many other pop acts in history, they simply refused to stand still, to rest on the laurels of a successful formula; as Victor Spinetti so succinctly puts it, they were like 'eternal students',[1] always keen to explore uncharted territories and, equally importantly, able to inspire a willingness in their audience to go with them. Love them or hate them, there is no getting away from the fact that the Beatles movies are, on several counts, probably the most 'deviant' series of British films to attain mainstream commercial success on an international level. That the frequently experimental formal style and avant-garde sensibilities of the films should have been, for the most part, so commercially successful also flies in the face of the popular and reductive film-theoretical assumption that British cinema must 'conform' to 'dominant' formal, ideological and distributive conventions in order to succeed in the international marketplace; and this, I believe, has been a significant contributory factor in the films' academic neglect. The films' success simply defies a formulaic answer, so rather than attempting to address the question, it has for the most part been ignored.

What, then, if anything, does the films' success 'prove'? A cynic would no doubt argue that it proves nothing, and maintain that the popularity of the Beatles' soundtracks 'sold' the films, and that the films were successful in spite of, rather than because of, their frequently radical formal or ideological properties. However, while few would deny that the Beatles were, because of their wealth and cultural status, in the relatively unique position of being able to experiment with hitherto untried formats and narrative structures, this argument fails to account for the fact that audiences could, had they so desired, have forsaken the films in the wake of their frequently hostile reviews, and bought into the group purely as recording artistes. This, as our study proves, did not happen, and I suspect that the films' success is at least partly due to their audiences' desire for – or at least receptiveness towards – experimentation and stylistic deviation. As I mentioned earlier, this certainly held true for the group's recording career, but whether this desire was unique to the reception of the Beatles' cinematic output remains an open question. However, if the films are placed in their historical context, it does seem that youthful sixties audiences in both Britain and America had a far greater tolerance and receptiveness towards stylistic deviation than those of the previous decade. Indeed, as Ken Hanke maintains, the 'open contempt for the mechanics of formal film-making' exuded by such films as *A Hard Day's Night* was so effective precisely because it provided an aesthetic and ideological alternative to the 'finely wrought Hollywood and ersatz-Hollywood British films' to which audiences had become accustomed.[2] They disposed of the 'well crafted dullness'[3] of much of what had gone before and, like the Marx Brothers in the early thirties, provided audiences with a sense of anarchic freedom which could not be obtained from the majority of contemporaneous British films.

However, whatever the exact reasons behind the films' success, there can be no denying that the Beatles movies have from a variety of perspectives exerted an enormous influence upon film and television and, at least as far as the pop musical genre is concerned, their influence has been so great that it is tentatively possible to posit pre-Beatles and post-Beatles analogies similar to those so frequently drawn by pop musicologists in relation to the group's recorded output. However, their impact also transcends their generic status, and I now want to take the films in turn and assess their influence in greater detail, from both a historical and a contemporary perspective.

Economically and stylistically, the success of the first two films, (and particularly *A Hard Day's Night*) had considerable impact on the British and American film and television industries. Firstly, the success of *A Hard Day's Night* contributed greatly to the influx of American capital into British film production throughout the decade; by 1967, 90 per cent of the funding for British movies was culled from the American majors. Indeed, as Robert Murphy has pointed out, the impact on the US market of such successful American investments as the Bond films, *Tom Jones* (1963) and *A Hard Day's Night* 'changed attitudes towards Britain, fostering a belief that London, rather than Paris or Rome or Hollywood, was the place in the world to make a film'.[4] Secondly, this investment had a considerable impact upon the increased distribution of British pop musicals and in turn upon the increasing profitability of the British recording industry in other territories, particularly America. As Kevin Donnelly has noted, 'The influx of American money and interest in Britain coincided with an unprecedented explosion of British popular music, the Beatles spearheading "the British invasion" of the US and Beatlemania signifying the power of the new pop music culture.'[5]

While it could be argued that the notorious 'British invasion' was beginning to take place in America (through the Beatles) before either they or any other British pop artiste had produced a successfully exportable film, it is certainly true that the Beatles' first two films, together with such imitative productions as *Catch Us If You Can* aka *Having A Wild Weekend* (1965) and *Ferry Cross the Mersey* (1964), played a significant yet frequently overlooked role in the dissemination of British pop throughout America. As we have discussed, the film and record industries fed off each other's successes and, although it is obviously rhetorical to speculate upon the fortunes of both the Beatles and British pop culture without the impact of *A Hard Day's Night*, and the subsequent imitations which its success encouraged, my suspicion is that the music industry would never have attained such a commanding position within America or, for that matter, have retained it within its homeland. This, of course, is a contentious issue, since the Beatles had already achieved an astonishing measure of national and international success prior to their forays into film. However, it is a truism that the 'flattery' of winning foreign endorsement (especially in America) frequently functions as a promotional stimulus for home audiences, and *A Hard Day's Night* was certainly central to the consolidation of the Beatles' and, by implication, British pop music's international approval abroad.

However, as well as compounding the 'British invasion' and heralding a spate of copycat movies, the first two Beatles films also exerted an enormous and lasting influence upon British and American television programmes. The most contemporaneously popular of these was undoubtedly the massively successful *Monkees* television show, which, from its inception in 1966, shamelessly exploited the style of the Lester movies (non-diegetic musical numbers interspersed with similar 'chase' scenarios), and featured a four-piece 'bubblegum' pop group whose coldly manufactured 'zaniness' was blatantly modelled on the Beatles' early presentation. *The Monkees*, however, came and went. The most lasting legacy of the Lester movies has undoubtedly been the effect their conceptual and illustrative employment of pop music has had on the visual language of the independently produced pop promo, something that the Beatles had pioneered from 1965 with the semi-diegetic Joe McGrath videos mentioned in Chapter Two, which was later taken to its logical conclusion in 1967 by both the Beatles in *Magical Mystery Tour* and the Swedish director Peter Goldmann, whose totally illustrative concept promos accompanied the 'Strawberry Fields Forever'/'Penny Lane' single. However, without the initial break with performance-oriented music heralded by the Lester films, the history of the pop video could well have developed very differently, and it is certainly possible that had the illustrative potential of pop music never been realized, the existence of the pop promo could well have been condemned to an obscure footnote in histories of sixties television. The Lester films established an aesthetic precedent which was to become central to a medium external to the one from which they evolved.

Although critically slated in its day, *Magical Mystery Tour* has also exerted considerable influence upon film and television. As well as its importance to the development of pop video, the film's radical rejection of conventional narrative logic helped to set an aesthetic precedent for subsequent pop movies such as the Monkees' *Head* (1968), Led Zeppelin's *The Song Remains the Same* (1976), Frank Zappa's *200 Motels* (1971) and the Who's *Tommy* (1975). Indeed, as Andy Medhurst notes, 'The sacrificing of narrative also meant the sacrificing of audiences, as the Beatles found to their cost with the bemused and hostile response which greeted *Magical Mystery Tour*. Yet after this radical midsixties break, there was no going back to the more accessible naiveties of *Live It Up* (1963) or *The Golden Disc* (1958), not, that is, if the resulting films were to have any shred of credibility.'[6] Indeed, the single greatest achievement of the film is that it played a key role in deinstitutionalizing a genre which, to all intents and purposes, had been largely institutionalized by the essentially conventional narrative form and predominantly conformist morality of previous pop musicals.

Apart from its key role in radicalizing the aesthetics of its genre, one might also argue that the formal and generic properties of *Magical Mystery Tour* influenced or at least predated other genres of film and television. Ian MacDonald, who like Medhurst is one of the few critics to recognize (albeit in passing) the film's importance, sees its concept as a prototype of the road movie genre which was inaugurated two years later with the release of *Easy Rider* (1969).[7] Moreover, I would maintain that elements of the film were influential on the style of later television comedy series such as *Marty* (1968–9), and *Monty Python's Flying Circus* (1969–74). Indeed, if the Beatles were inspired by John Cleese and Graham Chapman's early work, it might also be fair to acknowledge the formal influence of the Beatles film upon the Pythons. This is particularly evident in the second series of *Monty Python's Flying Circus* (1970), in which the constant use of the non-diegetic insert of the applauding crowd seems directly lifted from *Magical Mystery Tour*. Moreover, Terry Gilliam's use of surreal animation is also highly reminiscent of that used both in *Magical Mystery Tour* and *Yellow Submarine*, and in the second series, the 'Blackmail' sketch makes exactly the same use of the animated 'censored' sign. Some years later, when the comedy team had branched into full-length features, the Beatles' influence again remained apparent, and the grotesquely amusing exploding gourmand sketch in the Pythons' *The Meaning of Life* (1983) is highly reminiscent of the dream sequence in *Magical Mystery Tour* in which Lennon, dressed as a French waiter, is seen shovelling vast quantities of spaghetti on to Aunt Jessie's plate. That elements of *Magical Mystery Tour* should have been influential upon the Pythons is perhaps unsurprising. In the years following their split, former Beatles have been instrumental in supporting and collaborating with the Monty Python group. While Starr made a brief cameo appearance in a 1972 edition of the show, Harrison's film production company, Handmade, was responsible for funding a number of Python-related projects. The most notorious of these was undoubtedly their biblical satire, *The Life of Brian* (1979), which Harrison rescued when the controversial subject matter proved too much for EMI, the film's original financiers. He also appeared fleetingly in *The Rutles* (1978), the spoof Beatles television documentary written by Python stalwart Eric Idle and featuring music by Neil Innes of the Bonzo Dog Doo Dah Band.

Yellow Submarine was also influential in its own ways. As well as influencing the Python team and proving a remarkably successful forerunner to today's product-oriented movies, its chief contemporaneous contribution to British film culture lay in 'fostering a new subculture of what Mark Langer has called "animatophilia"'.[8] In a 1994 article for *Sight and Sound*, Leslie Felperin Sharman traces the influences of the film and maintains that it was instrumental in popularizing animation within art-house exhibition, its success encouraging programmers to buy in independent animated shorts which would otherwise have remained largely unseen outside the festival circuits.[9] Moreover, as Felperin Sharman maintains, the interest garnered by the film instigated a boom in animation production which resulted in *Yellow Submarine's* production studio, TVC, becoming 'one of the first large-scale training grounds for young film-makers, including Diane Jackson, who was later to make *The Snowman*'.[10]

However, in the final analysis, the most extraordinary aspect of the Beatles movies is that they continue to generate both interest and profit. Like the comedies of the Marx Brothers to which they were initially compared, the films still entertain and engage and, for the most part, amuse in a manner which seems to transcend their period. Indeed, the current popularity of the recently re-released Lester movies in the sell-through video market would seem to echo this notion, suggesting that the films have found new second and third generation audiences. As Ken Hanke has so rightly said of *A Hard Day's Night*, time has been kinder to the film than its original audience![11] For five films which were made with no intention of achieving a sense of permanence, they have dated far more gracefully than a number of their contemporaries, and there is no small irony in this. Lester said repeatedly in the sixties that he neither wanted nor expected his films to last.[12] Today, he is justifiably amused by the irony of this situation, and although modestly accepting that he finds it impossible to be objective about his own work, he concedes that on the odd occasions when he has reviewed his Beatles movies he finds them more 'endearingly representative of their period'[13] than a number of other contemporaneous films. So why have these five films worn so well? The reasons, I believe, are both complex and numerous.

Although the pop musical has become an increasingly dying genre, the formal language of the films lives on in the non-stop global video jukebox that is MTV. That there have been no textual developments of equal significance since the Beatles films has helped them to retain their youth. Granted, video-makers have discovered and exploited all manner of new effects and technologies, but the bottom line is that the fundamentally illustrative, concept-based aesthetic of non-performance initially established over thirty years ago by Lester is still very much in place.

Also of importance is the fact that the fashions and range of images popularized by the Beatles have become strongly integrated into the post-modern collage of styles which pervade contemporary pop culture. Indeed, while the psychedelic style sported by the group in *Magical Mystery Tour* (and by their cartoon counterparts in *Yellow Submarine*) has returned to the centre stage of indie pop fashion, the mid-sixties look of the *Help!/Revolver* period (corduroy and suede jackets, sunglasses and leather boots) has also become integral to the look of many pop bands; and to scrutinize the visual style of popular Beatles admirers Oasis is to witness a perfect synthesis of fashions culled from different periods of the Beatles' career and reassembled into a bricolage of styles which evokes a disturbingly schizophrenic sense of undifferentiated time. Likewise, the influence of the Beatles' music has never been so prominent. The so-called 'Britpop' revolution of the mid nineties has at its core of inspiration a nostalgic aping of the Beatles' abstract lyrical allusions and harmonic structures. Although a vast core of Beatles purists find the seemingly insatiable copyism of much contemporary pop to be at best tiresome, there is no doubt that the rise of 'Britpop' has, along with the well-timed *Anthology* series, refocused attention upon the Beatles' musical output for a generation who were not present at the time of its inception and dissemination.

That said, it seems that quite independently of the 'Britpop' revolution the films' soundtracks have retained an eternal youth, and this, I am sure, has been instrumental in the movies' longevity. George Martin's production was so advanced in its day, and has since been so perfectly and effectively conserved and enhanced by contemporary technology, that the 'sound' of the Beatles now seems far fresher than that of many of their contemporaries. Unlike the back catalogues of many of their sixties colleagues, the ravages of time have yet to catch up with the Beatles production; although most of their work was only recorded on four-track technology, the recordings have been lovingly remastered (with the cooperation of their original producer) and have retained a crystal-clear clarity of acoustic which has imbued them with a sense of permanence.

Beyond this clarity of sound lies the music itself, and it is ultimately the soundtrack compositions themselves which, more than anything else, have been central to the Beatles movies' evergreen popularity. The fact that they can be heard blaring from radios and televisions from Russia to Switzerland and from America to Australia has ensured that the music is very much part of the 'now'. Analysing the reasons behind the enduring success of any cultural artefact is by nature a speculative undertaking, but I would suggest that the central reason for the appeal of the Beatles is partly due to their durability. Unlike a vast number of their contemporaries (and Bob Dylan springs immediately to mind), the songs of Lennon, McCartney and Harrison ran the gamut of lyrical universal abstracts (love, anger, joy, sorrow, regret, etc.) in a manner which transcends contemporaneity. What is more, their musical approach to songwriting and arrangement encapsulated a far wider musical panorama than had, and indeed has, ever been attempted within pop. As well as developing the germ of their beloved rock and roll into new musical styles and experimenting and pioneering a range of recording techniques hitherto untried in pop, the Beatles were masters of musical pastiche, and this, in my opinion, is where their musical longevity most profoundly lies.

Songs written in pre-existing styles cannot, by their very nature, date as harshly as those which are not and, although they were not necessarily designed with this intention, many of the Beatles' soundtrack songs (and particularly those which appeared in the later films) succeed so well precisely for this reason. That the songs were often more memorable than those of the genres from which they initially derived is extraordinary (the Beatles always had an uncanny, infuriatingly brilliant knack of not only capturing the essence of their chosen targets, but somehow inexplicably 'improving' them), but the bottom line is that soundtrack songs such as 'And I Love Her', 'Yellow Submarine', 'Your Mother Should Know' or 'Let It Be' are (respectively) pastiches of the latin ballad, the children's nursery rhyme, the music-hall number and the hymn. Indeed, to my mind those who constantly explain the Beatles' current 'revival' as the result of so much 'nostalgia' fail to see the whole picture; whatever else constituted their vast contribution to music, an important ingredient of their original underlying appeal across the ages was partly nostalgic in the first instance.

With the Beatles' official split in 1970 came the end of the most successful pop group of all time. Significantly perhaps, their demise also paralleled the decline of large scale investment into British cinema. The degree to which the Beatles' split influenced this decline is clearly unquantifiable, but while it has often been rather reductively explained as the result of the internal schisms and declining returns which characterized such late sixties productions as *Casino Royale* (1967), *Performance* (1968, not released until 1970), *Modesty Blaise* (1967) and *The Charge of the Light Brigade* (1968), only the most foolhardy of commentators would ignore the direct and indirect influence of the group's split on this phenomenon. On a purely cinematic level, their demise meant that there was one less group of highly bankable British stars for the picking. Yet if the Beatles had never set foot in a movie studio, I suspect their split would still have made an impact on foreign investment into British film.

After all, at the epicentre of America's sustained investment in British cinema was not only the homegrown talents of Britain's film industry, but from a broader perspective, the country's fashionableness as a mecca of exportable pop culture, which also encapsulated fashion design, photography, the fine arts and, perhaps most importantly, pop music (most importantly, because pop music was the most widely disseminated and 'inescapable' of these media, especially in America, where from 1964 it reverberated around the country as a stern and omnipotent warning to financiers that Britain's new-found cultural fashionability was not to be ignored). Throughout the sixties, the Beatles were so much the nucleus of the cultural revolution that it is almost impossible to imagine it ever having happened without them. Although America's first major investments of the decade predated the Beatles' international success by a whisker (for example, United Artists' investment in *Dr No* occurred in the same year as the Beatles' first British hit single), one might argue that their international popularity was the single most important factor in sustaining Britain's cultural credibility throughout the decade. Indeed, as Dick Lester maintains, 'It is hard to over-estimate the grip of the fab four on the popular imagination of the time.'[14] After all, directly or otherwise, the group were key players in virtually every successfully exported and/or innovative popular artistic medium of their age, not only as film stars and film-makers, but as models for the newly emerging Carnaby Street fashions, as photographic subjects for David Bailey, Dezo Hoffmann, Richard Avedon and Robert Freeman, as key conspirators in the marriage of fine art and pop, and of course as writers and performers of the most widely exported and distributed music in history. Discussing the withdrawal of American funding in the early seventies, the group's American film producer Walter Shenson explained that 'this place no longer makes news that is of interest to the world. When society is under stress or going through change, the outlines of what's happening are unfamiliar and exciting and the artists are under pressure to react to it all. When we are over-familiar with what has been happening, all that is left is a hangover.'[15] Some would argue that Britain has never fully recovered.

Although the sixties have long been canonized as something of a 'golden age' in British film, the fact remains that the majority of the Beatles films have received less critical coverage and analysis than they deserve, despite their unwaning appeal. There will, I hope, come a time when that appeal will be matched by a critical interest which will, in turn, engender a historical recognition which eventually parallels that of their recorded output. My sincere hope is that this book will go some way towards stimulating interest and debate about these most overlooked and undervalued gems of British cinema, in my opinion the most thoughtful, anarchic and joyous series of pop movies of the decade that spawned them.

Notes

1. Victor Spinetti, interviewed by author, 29 April 1996.
2. Hanke, 1989, p. 214.
3. Ibid., p. 213.
4. Murphy, 1992, p. 114.
5. Kevin Donnelly, 'Music in *A Hard Day's Night*', unpublished PhD thesis, 'Pop Music in British Cinema', University of East Anglia.
6. Medhurst, in Romney and Wootton (eds), 1995, pp. 68–9.
7. MacDonald, 1994, p. 204.
8. Felperin Sharman, 1994, p. 15.
9. Ibid.
10. Ibid.
11. Hanke, 1989, p. 213.
12. Melly, 1970, p. 167.
13. Dick Lester, interviewed by author, 26 March 1996.
14. Hollywood, UK (BBC)
15. Walker, 1986, pp. 450–1.

Bibliography
Principal Books and Articles

Note: Dates and publishers listed below refer to the editions of the books used by the author. Although some are first editions, many of the works cited are paperback reprints and/or revised editions of previously published works. Furthermore, the bibliography includes only those articles which have been exceptionally useful to the work either as a source for quotations or for historical information. Full details of articles mentioned only in passing are to be found in the endnotes for each chapter.

Aldridge, Alan (1981) *Phantasia*. London: Cape.

Allen, Don (ed.) (1979) *The Book of the Cinema*. London: Artists House.

Atkins, Robert (1993) *Art Spoke: a Guide to Modern Ideas, Movements and Buzzwords 1848–1944*. New York: Abbeville Press.

Barrow, Tony (1987a) 'How the Magical Mystery Tour Began', *Beatles Monthly Book*, no. 137, September 1987, pp. 5–9.

Barrow, Tony (1987b) 'Filming the Magical Mystery Tour', *Beatles Monthly Book*, no. 138, October 1987, pp. 4–9.

Barrow, Tony (1993a) 'The Story Behind A Hard Day's Night', *Beatles Monthly Book*, no. 209, September 1993, pp. 5–11.

Barrow, Tony (1993b) 'The Story of Yellow Submarine', *Beatles Monthly Book*, no. 204, April 1993. pp. 8–13.

Beck, Spencer, J. (ed.) (1994) *Variety Book of Movie Lists*. London: Hamlyn.

Bennahum, David (1991) *The Beatles After the Break-Up*. London: Omnibus.

Berger, John (1972) *Ways of Seeing*. Harmondsworth: Penguin.

Blake, John (1981) *All You Needed Was Love*. London: Hamlyn.

Booker, Christopher (1970) *The Neophiliacs*. London: Fontana.

Bordwell, David, Staiger, Janet and Thompson, Kristin (1991) *The Classical Hollywood Cinema: Film Style and Mode of Production to 1960*. London: Routledge.

Bordwell, David and Thompson, Kristin (1979) *Film Art*. London: Addison-Wesley.

Bowman, David (1972) 'Scenarios for the Revolution in Pepperland', *Journal of Popular Film and Television*, vol. 1, pt. 3, 1972, pp. 173–84.

Braun, Michael (1964) *Love Me Do: the Beatles' Progress*. Harmondsworth: Penguin.

Brown, Peter and Gaines, Steven (1984) *The Love You Make*. London: Pan.

Buskin, Richard (1994) *Beatle Crazy! Memories and Memorabilia*. London: Salamander.

Canemaker, John (1986/7) 'The Dunning Touch', *Sightlines*, vol. 20, pt. 2, pp. 22–5.

Clayson, Alan (1991) *Ringo Starr: Straight Man or Joker?* London: Sidgwick and Jackson.

Cohn, Nik (1967) 'The Love Generation', *Queen*, 19 July 1967, pp. 27–9.

Collins, Jim, Radner, Hilary and Collins, Ava (eds.) (1993) *Film Theory Goes to the Movies*. London: Routledge.

Connolly, Ray (1981) *John Lennon 1940–1980*. London: Fontana.

Cott, Jonathan and Dalton, David (1970) 'Daddy Has Gone Away Now', *Rolling Stone*, 9 July 1970, pp. 20–3.

Davies, Hunter (1969) *The Beatles*. London: Mayflower.

Davis, Arthur (1994) *The Beatles: Quote Unquote*. Bristol: Parragon.

Dawabarn, Bob (1968) 'Why All the Mystery over the Magical Mystery Tour?', *Melody Maker*, 6 January 1968, p. 5.

Dilello, Richard (1972) *The Longest Cocktail Party*. London: Charisma.

Doggett, Peter (1995) 'The Big Beat on the Big Screen', *Record Collector*, no.187, March 1995, pp. 46–9.

Doherty, Thomas (1988) *Teenagers and Teenpics: the Juvenilization of American Movies in the 1950's*. London: Unwin.

Dwoskin, Stephen (1975) *Film Is*. London: Peter Owen.

Evans, Mal and Aspinall, Neil (1967) 'Magical Mystery Tour', *Beatles Monthly Book*, no. 53, December 1967, pp. 6–13.

Evans, Mal and Aspinall, Neil (1968) 'How the Magical EPs Were Made', *Beatles Monthly Book*, no. 54, January 1968, pp. 8–11.

Evans, Mike (1984) *The Art of the Beatles*. London: Anthony Blond in association with Merseyside City Council.

Ewing, Elizabeth (1974) *History of Twentieth Century Fashion*. London: Batsford.

Friede, Goldie, Titone, Robin and Weiner, Sue (1981) *The Beatles A-Z*. London: Methuen.

Frith, Simon (1978) *The Sociology of Rock*. London: 1978.

Frith, Simon and Horne, Howard (1987) *Art into Pop*. London: Methuen.

Gambaccini, Paul (1976) *Paul McCartney in His Own Words*. London: Omnibus.

Gambaccini, Paul, Read, Mike, Rice, Jo and Rice, Tim (1982) *The Guinness Book of British Hit Singles*. Enfield: Guinness.

Gambaccini, Paul and Rice, Jo and Rice, Tim (1985) *The Guinness Book of British Hit Albums*. Enfield: Guinness.

Giuliano, Geoffrey (1991) *Dark Horse: the Private Life of George Harrison*. New York: Plume.

Giuliano, Geoffrey and Giuliano, Brenda (1994) *The Lost Beatles Interviews*. London: Virgin.

Green, Jonathon (1988) *Days in the Life: Voices from the English Underground 1961–1971*. London: Heinemann.

Grossman, Henry (1967) 'The Beatles: Their New Incarnation', *Time*, 22 September 1967, pp. 56–8.

Hamilton, George Heard (1985) *Painting and Sculpture in Europe 1880–1940*. London: Pelican.

Hanke, Ken (1989) 'The British Film Invasion of the 1960s', *Films in Review*, vol. 40, pt. 4, April 1989, pp. 213–19.

Harry, Bill (1984) *Beatlemania: an Illustrated Filmography*. London: Virgin.

Hertsgaard, Mark (1995) *A Day in the Life: the Music and Artistry of the Beatles*. London: Macmillan.

Hewison, Robert (1986) *Too Much: Art and Society in the Sixties*. London: Methuen.

Hutchinson, Roger (1992) *High Sixties: the Summers of Riot and Love*. Edinburgh: Mainstream.

Johnson, Derek (1967) 'Most Way-Out Beatles Ever', *New Musical Express*, 11 February 1967, p. 6.

Kelly, Freda (1967) 'Four Points of View of Magical Mystery Tour', *Beatles Monthly Book*, no. 52, December 1967, pp. 6–11.

Kozinn, Allan (1995) *The Beatles*. London: Phaidon.

Kureishi, Hanif (1991) *London Kills Me*. London: Faber.

Lahr, John (1980) *Prick up Your Ears: The Biography of Joe Orton*. Harmondsworth: Penguin.

Leech, Kenneth (1973) *Youthquake: the Growth of a Counter-Culture through Two Decades*. London: Sheldon.

Lewisohn, Mark (1989) *The Complete Beatles Recording Sessions*. London: Hamlyn.

Lewisohn, Mark (1992) *The Complete Beatles Chronicle*. London: Pyramid.

McCabe, Peter and Schonfeld, Robert (1972) *Apple to the Core*. Ontario: Pocket.

MacDonald, Ian (1994) *Revolution in the Head: the Beatles' Records and the Sixties*. London: Fourth Estate.

Madow, Stuart and Sobul, Jeff (1992) *The Colour of Your Dreams*. Pittsburgh: Dorrance.

Martin, George with Hornsby, Jeremy (1979) *All You Need Is Ears*. New York: St. Martins Press.

Martin, George (1995) *The Summer of Love*. London: Pan.

Marwick, Arthur (1990) *British Society Since 1945*. Harmondsworth: Penguin.

Mellers, Wilfred (1973) *Twilight of the Gods: The Beatles in Retrospect*. London: Faber.

Melly, George (1970) *Revolt into Style*. London: Allen Lane.

Miles (1978) *The Beatles in Their Own Words*. London: Omnibus.

Miles (1980) *John Lennon in His Own Words*. London: Omnibus.

Murphy, Robert (1992) *Sixties British Cinema*. London: BFI.

Neville, Richard (1970) *Playpower*. London: Paladin.

Neville, Richard (1995) *The Hippie Hippie Shake*. London: Bloomsbury.

Norman, Philip (1981) *Shout!*. London: Elm Tree.

Perry, George (1986) *The Life of Python*. London: Pavilion.

Rogan, Johnny (1989) *Starmakers and Svengalis*. London: Futura.

Romney, Jonathan and Wootton, Adrian (eds) (1995) *Celluloid Jukebox: Popular Music in the Movies Since the 50s*. London: BFI.

Sharman, Leslie Felperin (1994) 'Animatophilia', *Sight and Sound*, 'Art into Film' supplement, July 1994, pp. 14–15.

Sheff, David and Golson, G. Barry (1982) *The Playboy Interviews with John Lennon and Yoko Ono*. Sevenoaks: NEL.

Somach, Denny, Somach, Kathleen and Muni, Scott (1990) *Ticket to Ride*. London: Futura.

Spence, Helen (1981) *The Beatles Forever*. New Maldon: Colour Books.

Staiger, Janet (1992) *Interpreting Films*. Princeton: Princeton University Press.

Stangos, Nikos (ed.) (1974) *Concepts of Modern Art*. London: Thames and Hudson.

Stannard, Neville (1982) *The Long and Winding Road*. London: Virgin.

Stannard, Neville (1984) *Working Class Heroes*. London: Virgin.

Taylor, Alistair and Roberts, Martin (1988) *Yesterday: the Beatles Remembered*. London: Sidgwick and Jackson.

Thompson, Thomas (1967) 'The New Far-Out Beatles', *Life*, 16 June 1967, pp. 101–6.

Tyler, Parker (1969) *Underground Films*. New York: Grove.

Waldberg, Patrick (1967) *Surrealism*. London: Thames and Hudson.

Walker, Alexander (1986) *Hollywood, England*. London: Harrap.

Wenner, Jan (1973) *Lennon Remembers*. Harmondsworth: Penguin.

Wheen, Francis (1982) *The Sixties*. London: Century/Channel 4.

Wiener, Jon (1985) *Come Together: John Lennon in His Time*. London: Faber.

Wolfe, Tom (1989) *The Electric Kool-Aid Acid Test*. London: Black Swan.

Further Reading

Film

Books which deal exclusively with the Beatles' film career are virtually non-existent. However, three books should be consulted for their informed approach to the films. Lewisohn's *Complete Beatles Chronicle* provides an indispensable day-to-day account of the Beatles' entire career and is, without doubt, the most informed source of factual information on the group written to date. Walker's *Hollywood, England* contains a riveting commentary on the making of *A Hard Day's Night*, and Harry's *Beatlemania* contains interesting information on the group's movies and television appearances.

Music

Mark Lewisohn's *Complete Beatles Recording Sessions* is a first-rate diary of the group's recording endeavours for those seeking factual information regarding the production of the films' soundtracks. Neville Stannard's *Long and Winding Road* also provides an excellent discography. For a more critical approach, MacDonald's *Revolution in the Head* is highly recommended.

The Beatles' Career

Apart from Lewisohn's day-by-day chronicle, Philip Norman's *Shout!* provides an informed and gripping narrative. Davies' *The Beatles* is also a well-written account of the Beatles' history, and contains fascinating interviews with all four members of the group. Finally, for an informed and fascinating insight into the Beatles' position within sixties pop culture, see Melly's extraordinary *Revolt into Style*.

The Beatles Filmography

A Hard Day's Night (1964)

Production Company: Proscenium Films; Directed by: Richard Lester.

Synopsis: The Beatles, accompanied by their entourage, travel south to London where they are to appear on a television show. On arrival at the show's studios, Ringo is led astray by Paul's grandfather and there then ensues a series of attempts to find Ringo before the show begins. Eventually he returns and the Beatles perform to an ecstatic audience before departing in a helicopter for their next venue.

Cast: The Beatles; Wilfred Brambell: Grandfather; Norman Rossington: Norm; John Junkin: Shake; Victor Spinetti: Television Director; Kenneth Haigh: Shirt Advertising Man; Anna Quayle: Millie; Derek Guyler: Policeman; Richard Vernon: Man on Train; Michael Trubshawe: Club Manager; Eddie Malin: Waiter; Bridget Armstrong, Roger Avon, Lionel Blair, John Bluthal, Patti Boyd.

Credits: Richard Lester: Director; Walter Shenson: Producer; Denis O'Dell: Associate Producer; John D. Merriman: Assistant Director; Alun Owen: Scriptwriter; Gilbert Taylor: Photography; John Jympson: Editor; Ray Simm: Art Director; Julie Harris: Costumes; George Martin: Musical Director; Robert Freeman: Titles; H.L Bird, Stephen Dalby: Sound Recording.

Running time: 85 mins; Length: 7650 ft or 2333 m.

Black-and-white.

Help! (1965)

Production Company: Walter Shenson Films/ Subafilms; Directed by: Richard Lester.

Synopsis: Upon the realization that Ringo is wearing a holy sacrificial ring known as Kaili, the members of a mysterious Eastern cult chase the Beatles through locations in the Bahamas, London and Austria in an attempt to obtain the ring, which has become stuck to Ringo's finger. In their efforts to remove it, Ringo and the other members of the group consult Professor Foot and his apprentice, Algernon, who, like the members of the Eastern cult, seek to take control of the powerful ring.

Cast: The Beatles; Leo McKern: Clang; Eleanor Bron: Ahme; Victor Spinetti: Foot; Roy Kinnear: Algernon; Patrick Cargill: Superintendent; John Bluthal: Blutha; Alfie Bass: Doorman; Warren Mitchell: Abdul; Peter Copley: Jeweller; Bruce Lacey: Lawnmower.

Credits: Richard Lester: Director; Walter Shenson: Producer; John Pellatt: Production Manager; Clive Reed: Assistant Director; Marc Behm, Charles Wood: Scriptwriters; David Watkin: Photography; Robert Freeman: Colour Consultant and Titles; John Victor Smith: Editor; Ray Simm: Art Director; Ken Thorne: Musical Director; Barrie Vince: Musical Editor; Julie Harris: Costumes; H.L. Bird, Stephen Dalby, Don Challis: Sound; Bill Blunden: Sound Editor.

Running time: 92 mins; Length: 8280 ft or 2525 m.

Colour.

Magical Mystery Tour (TVM 1967)

Production Company: Apple Films; Directed by: The Beatles.

Synopsis: Surreal/psychedelic musical adventure comedy in which the Beatles, along with a mixture of bizarre characters, board a bus and set off upon a magical mystery tour. Along the way, they stop at an army barracks, a strip club and an Italian restaurant, eventually ending up at a Busby Berkeley-style film set, where the group perform the show's finale song, 'Your Mother Should Know'.

Cast: The Beatles; George Claydon: Little George; Ivor Cutler: Buster Bloodvessel; Shirley Evans: The Accordionist; Nat Jackley: Happy Nat; Nicola: Little Girl; Jessie Robbins: Aunty Jessie; Victor Spinetti: Army Sergeant; Maggie Wright: Starlet; Derek Royle: Jolly Jimmy; Jan Carson: Stripper; Mandy Weet: Miss Winters; The Bonzo Dog Do Dah Band: Themselves.

Credits: The Beatles: Directors/ Producers; Denis O' Dell: Production; Gavrik Losey: Assistant; Andrew Burkin: First Assistant Director; Aubrey Dewar, Tony Busbridge, Daniel Lacamore, Mike Sarason: Photography; Ringo Starr: Director of Photography; Roy Benson: Editor; Roger Graham: Design; Keith Liddiard: Design; Michael Lax: Sound; Gordon Daniel: Sound Editor.

Running Time: 54 mins.

Colour.

Yellow Submarine (1968)

Production Company: King Features Entertainment/Subafilms/TVC/ Apple Films; Directed by: George Dunning.

Synopsis: Following the attacks of the ruthless Blue Meanies, the peace-loving inhabitants of Pepperland are left frozen in motionless misery. On the advice of Old Fred, the community's ruler, Young Fred flees in a submarine for help. After enlisting the help of the Beatles (who in turn enlist the help of a lovable cartoon animal called Jeremy Boob), the posse return to Pepperland where, taking on the guise of a frozen brass band ensemble (Sergeant Pepper's Lonely Hearts Club band), the Beatles defeat the oppressive regime of 'blueness' by using music as a weapon to restore the happiness and order of Pepperland. Defeated, the evil regime sees the error of its ways and joins with the newly restored order, vowing to build a better and happier world.

Cast of Voices: John Clive, Geoffrey Hughes, Lance Percival, Paul Angelis, Dick Emery.

Credits: George Dunning: Director; Al Brodax: Producer; Mary Ellen Stewart: Associate Producer; John Coates: Production Supervisor; Lee Minoff, Erich Segal, Jack Mendelsohn, Al Brodax: Scriptwriters; Lee Minoff: Original Story, inspired by the song by John Lennon and Paul McCartney; John Williams: Camera; Jack Stokes, Bob Balser: Animation Directors; Alan Ball, Hester Coblentz, Rich Cox, Arthur Cuthbert, Cam Ford, Ann Jolliffe, Tom Halley, Jim Hiltz, Arthur Humberstone, Reg Lodge, Terry Moesker, Mike Pocock, Edric Radage, Mike Stuart: Animators; Chris Cannter: Special Effects Animator; Helen Jones, Corona Mayer, Janet Hosie, Margaret Geddes: Head Checkers; Millie McMillan, Alison De Vere: Background; Brian J. Bishop: Editor; Heinz Edelmann, John Cramer, Gordon Harrison: Designers; Charles Jenkins: Special Effects; George Martin: Musical Director; Donald Cohen, Ken Rolls: Sound.

Running time: 87 mins; Length: 7830 ft or 2388 m.

Colour.

Let It Be (1969, released 1970)

Production Company: Apple Films; Directed by: Michael Lindsay-Hogg.

Synopsis: The Beatles assemble to rehearse some new songs, to run through some old rock and roll standards and, eventually, to play an impromptu concert on the roof of the Apple building in Savile Row. As they perform the concert, a number of people below comment on the group and their music and, reacting to the noise, the police enter the Apple building and climb to the roof where the concert is eventually called to a halt.

Cast: The Beatles.

Credits: Michael Lindsay-Hogg: Director; The Beatles: Executive Producers; Neil Aspinall: Producer; Anthony B. Richmond: Photography; Tony Lenny: Editor; Peter Sutton: Sound.

Running time: 81 mins; Length: 7290 ft or 2223 m.

Colour.

Discography of the Beatles' British Film Soundtrack Albums

This discography contains listings for the Beatles' soundtrack albums together with their British catalogue numbers for CD recordings. However, a couple of important points should be made. Firstly, the songs on side two of the first three listed releases are not featured in the films at all, and secondly, the soundtrack album for *Let It Be* contains, for the most part, remixed and/or rerecorded versions of songs performed in the film. It should also be pointed out that the songs listed on side two of the *Yellow Submarine* soundtrack are performed by the George Martin Orchestra.

A Hard Day's Night (CDP 7464372, Mono)

Original British LP issue: 10 July 1964.

Side One	*Side Two*
A Hard Day's Night	Any Time at All
I Should Have Known Better	I'll Cry Instead
If I Fell	Things We Said Today
I'm Happy Just to Dance with You	When I Get Home
And I Love Her	You Can't Do That
Tell Me Why	I'll Be Back
Can't Buy Me Love	

All songs by Lennon/McCartney. Produced by George Martin.

Help! (CDP 7464392, Stereo)

Original British LP issue: 6 August 1965.

Side One	*Side Two*
Help!	Act Naturally
The Night Before	It's Only Love
You've Got to Hide Your Love Away	You Like Me Too Much
I Need You	Tell Me What You See
Another Girl	I've Just Seen a Face
You're Going to Lose That Girl	Yesterday
Ticket to Ride	Dizzy Miss Lizzy

Songs by Lennon/McCartney except 'Act Naturally' (Morrison/Russell), 'Dizzy Miss Lizzy' (Williams), 'I Need You' (Harrison) and 'You Like Me Too Much' (Harrison). Produced by George Martin.

Magical Mystery Tour (CDP 7480622, Stereo)

Side One originally issued in Britain on double EP format, 8 December 1967.

Side One	*Side Two*
Magical Mystery Tour	Hello Goodbye
The Fool on the Hill	Strawberry Fields Forever
Flying	Penny Lane
Blue Jay Way	Baby, You're a Rich Man
Your Mother Should Know	All You Need is Love
I Am the Walrus	

Songs by Lennon/McCartney except 'Flying' (Lennon/McCartney/Harrison/Starr) and 'Blue Jay Way' (Harrison). Produced by George Martin.

Yellow Submarine (CDP 7464452, Stereo)

Original British LP issue: 17 January 1969.

Side One	*Side Two*
Yellow Submarine	Pepperland
Only a Northern Song	Sea of Time
All Together Now	Sea of Holes
Hey Bulldog	Sea of Monsters
It's All Too Much	March of the Meanies
All You Need is Love	Pepperland Laid Waste
	Yellow Submarine in Pepperland

All songs on side one by Lennon/McCartney except 'Only a Northern Song' (Harrison) and 'It's All Too Much' (Harrison). Produced by George Martin.

Let It Be (CDP 7464472, Stereo)

Original British LP issue: 8 May 1970.

Side One	*Side Two*
Two of Us	I've Got a Feeling
Dig a Pony	One After 909
Across the Universe	The Long and Winding Road
I Me Mine	For You Blue
Dig It	Get Back
Let It Be	
Maggie Mae	

Songs by Lennon/McCartney except 'I Me Mine' (Harrison) and 'For You Blue' (Harrison). Produced by Phil Spector.

Index